W9-AMR-004

STOPPARD

in an hour

BY MIKHAIL ALEXEEFF

SUSAN C. MOORE, SERIES EDITOR

PLAYWRIGHTS in an hour
know the playwright, love the play

IN AN HOUR BOOKS • HANOVER, NEW HAMPSHIRE • INANHOURBOOKS.COM
AN IMPRINT OF SMITH AND KRAUS PUBLISHERS, INC • SMITHANDKRAUS.COM

With grateful thanks to Carl R. Mueller, whose fascinating introductions to his translations of the Greek and German playwrights provided inspiration for this series.

Published by In an Hour Books
an imprint of Smith and Kraus, Inc.
177 Lyme Road, Hanover, NH 03755
inanhourbooks.com SmithandKraus.com

Know the playwright, love the play.

In an Hour, In a Minute, and Theater IQ are registered trademarks of
In an Hour Books.

Front cover design by Dan Mehling, dmehling@gmail.com
Text design by Kate Mueller, Electric Dragon Productions
Book production by Dede Cummings Design, DCDesign@sover.net

ISBN-13: 978-1-936232-27-7
ISBN-10: 1-936232-27-8
Library of Congress Control Number: 2009943235

CONTENTS

Why Playwrights in an Hour?   v
by Carl R. Mueller

Introduction   vii
by Robert Brustein

Stoppard: IN A MINUTE   ix

Stoppard: HIS WORKS   x

ONSTAGE WITH STOPPARD:
Introducing Colleagues and
Contemporaries of Tom Stoppard   xiii

STOPPARD: In an Hour   1

APPENDICES

Dramatic Moments from the Major Plays   39

Stoppard: THE READING ROOM   67

Awards: "And the winner is . . ."   70

INDEX   74

Why Playwrights in an Hour?

This new series by Smith and Kraus Publishers titled Playwrights in an Hour has a dual purpose for being: one academic, the other general. For the general reader, this volume, as well as the many others in the series, offers in compact form the information needed for a basic understanding and appreciation of the works of each volume's featured playwright. Which is not to say that there don't exist volumes on end devoted to each playwright under consideration. But inasmuch as few are blessed with enough time to read the splendid scholarship that is available, a brief, highly focused accounting of the playwright's life and work is in order. The central feature of the series, a thirty- to forty-page essay, integrates the playwright into the context of his or her time and place. The volumes, though written to high standards of academic integrity, are accessible in style and approach to the general reader as well as to the student and, of course, to the theater professional and theatergoer. These books will serve for the brushing up of one's knowledge of a playwright's career, to the benefit of theater work or theatergoing. The Playwrights in an Hour series represents all periods of Western theater: Aeschylus to Shakespeare to Wedekind to Ibsen to Williams to Beckett, and on to the great contemporary playwrights who continue to offer joy and enlightenment to a grateful world.

Carl R. Mueller
School of Theater, Film, and Television
Department of Theater
University of California, Los Angeles

Introduction

Yeats once said that writers who argue with themselves create poetry while those who argue with others create rhetoric. Tom Stoppard represents a third development — a writer who argues with the arguers, and creates commentary. After the socially engaged, angry young playwrights of the fifties, Stoppard led the next postmodern stage of British drama. By adding both an epigrammatic style and a scholarly approach to theater, he moved it backward in form and forward in subject matter.

One can only speculate about the reasons for these contradictory literary directions. Some have surmised that Tom Stoppard, born Tomas Straussler in Czechoslovakia and the stepson of a British army major, had an identity crisis when he learned later in life that his parents were Jewish. Others have suggested that Stoppard's fondness for academicism — he often resembles an Elizabethan "university wit" — is a common quality of autodidacts (Stoppard never attended university). Whatever the case, from the moment Stoppard burst upon the English stage with his play about two footnote characters in *Hamlet* called *Rosencrantz and Guildenstern Are Dead*, indebted to *Waiting for Godot*, he was essentially writing dissertations about existing academic, scientific, literary, and political icons.

If this made a few spectators feel like retired learners taking refresher courses at an Adult Extension School, it also had the advantage of introducing audiences to arcane subjects of considerable interest. In the last three decades, for example, Stoppard has reflected on A. J. Ayer and logical positivism (*Jumpers*); on Tristan Tzara, Vladimir Lenin, James Joyce, and literary-political exile (*Travesties*); on Byron, Hobbes, Newton, Fermat, and hydroponic gardening (*Arcadia*); and on A. E. Houseman, Walter Pater, Benjamin Jowett, Oscar Wilde, and male love (*The Invention of Love*). In a more recent offering, the epic nine-hour trilogy called *The Coast of Utopia*, Stoppard covers the entire history of Russian Idealism, as represented by six major figures of the pre-revolutionary intelligentsia.

Eric Bentley once wrote a book called *The Playwright as Thinker*. How would he have categorized Tom Stoppard? The Playwright as Research Professor?

Stoppard researches his subjects with considerable learning and wit, not to mention exemplary literary skill. What critics have found missing is the pulse and heartbeat of genuine feeling — though this is less of a problem in a play like *The Real Thing* and a movie like *Shakespeare in Love*. Aristotle believed that the highest purpose of tragedy was to inspire in the spectator pity and terror for the characters' fate. Stoppard's work more often produces awe and admiration for the playwright's wit. This was also the achievement of such inspired comic writers as Oscar Wilde and Noël Coward, and sometimes Bernard Shaw, whose tradition Stoppard seems to be tapping. Stoppard's originality consists in combining that witty tradition with self-conscious intellectual commentary, and that is his chief contribution to post-modern drama.

Robert Brustein
Founding Director of the Yale and American Repertory Theatres
Distinguished Scholar in Residence, Suffolk University
Senior Research Fellow, Harvard University

Stoppard

IN A MINUTE

AGE	DATE	
—	1937	**Enter Tom Stoppard, born Tomas Straussler.**
1	1938	Thornton Wilder — *Our Town*
2	1939	First American food-stamp program begins in Rochester, New York.
4	1941	Orson Welles makes his debut in *Citizen Kane.*
6	1943	Shoe rationing begins in the U.S.
8	1945	General George Patton's 3rd U.S. Army liberates Czechoslovakia.
12	1949	George Orwell — *Nineteen Eighty-Four*
14	1951	UN Headquarters opens for business in New York City.
16	1953	Samuel Beckett — *Waiting for Godot*
19	1956	John Osborne — *Look Back in Anger*
20	1957	Soviets launch Sputnik 1, first satellite to orbit Earth.
22	1959	Fidel Castro seizes power in Cuba from General Fulgencio Batista.
25	1962	Edward Albee — *Who's Afraid of Virginia Woolf?*
27	1964	The Beatles top the charts in the U.S. and the UK
29	**1966**	**Tom Stoppard — *Rosencrantz and Guildenstern Are Dead***
31	1968	The Roman Catholic Church condemns birth control in *Humanae Vitae.*
35	**1972**	**Tom Stoppard — *Jumpers***
36	1973	Pink Floyd — *Dark Side of the Moon*
37	**1974**	**Tom Stoppard — *Travesties***
39	1976	Apple Computer opens for business in Cupertino, California.
40	1977	Publication of Charter 77 in Czechoslovakia invigorates dissidents.
41	**1978**	**Tom Stoppard — *Night and Day***
42	1979	Ayatollah Khomeini overthrows the Shah of Iran and forms a theocracy.
45	**1982**	**Tom Stoppard — *The Real Thing***
50	1987	Tom Wolfe — *Bonfire of the Vanities*
51	**1988**	**Tom Stoppard — *Hapgood***
52	1989	The Velvet Revolution frees Czechoslovakia from the communist regime.
61	**1998**	**Tom Stoppard co-writes *Shakespeare in Love* with Marc Norman.**
66	2003	Mars and Earth close to 35 million miles apart, nearest in 60 thousand years.
69	**2006**	**Tom Stoppard — *Rock 'n' Roll***

A snapshot of the playwright's world. From historical events to pop-culture and the literary landscape of the time, this brief list catalogues events that directly or indirectly impacted the playwright's writing. Play citations refer to premiere dates.

Stoppard

HIS WORKS

STAGE PLAYS

The Gamblers

Rosencrantz and Guildenstern Are Dead

The Real Inspector Hound

Enter a Free Man

After Magritte

Dogg's Our Pet

Jumpers

Travesties

Dirty Linen

New-Found-Land

The Fifteen-Minute Hamlet

Every Good Boy Deserves Favour

Night and Day

Dogg's Hamlet, Cahoot's Macbeth

The Real Thing

Hapgood

Arcadia

Indian Ink

The Invention of Love

Voyage: The Coast of Utopia Part I

Shipwreck: The Coast of Utopia Part II

Salvage: The Coast of Utopia Part III

Rock 'n' Roll

This section presents a complete list of the playwright's works in chronological order.

ADAPTATIONS

Tango
The House of Bernarda Alba
Undiscovered Country
On the Razzle
The Love for Three Oranges
Rough Crossing
Dalliance
Largo Desolato
The Seagull
Henry IV
Heroes

RADIO PLAYS (Airing premiere)

The Dissolution of Dominic Boot
"M" Is for Moon Among Other Things
If You're Glad, I'll be Frank
Albert's Bridge
Where Are They Now?
Artist Descending a Staircase
The Dog It Was That Died
In the Native State
On Dover Beach

TELEPLAYS

A Separate Peace
A Paragraph for Mr. Blake
Teeth
Another Moon Called Earth
Neutral Ground
Three Men in a Boat
The Boundary
Professional Foul
Squaring the Circle
Poodle Springs

SCREENPLAYS

The Romantic Englishwoman
Despair
The Human Factor
Brazil
Empire of the Sun
The Russia House
Billy Bathgate
Shakespeare in Love (with Marc Norman)
Enigma

NOVEL

Lord Malquist and Mr Moon

Onstage with Stoppard

Introducing Colleagues and Contemporaries of Tom Stoppard

 THEATER

Arthur C. Clarke, English author
Joe Orton, English playwright
Peter O'Toole, English actor
Harold Pinter, English playwright
Sam Shepard, American playwright and actor
Maggie Smith, English actress
August Wilson, American playwright
Lanford Wilson, American playwright

 ARTS

Syd Barrett, English musician
Bob Dylan, American musician
Mick Jagger, English musician
John Lennon, English musician
Paul McCartney, English musician
John Peel, English DJ and radio personality
Keith Richards, English musician
Andy Warhol, American pop artist

 FILM

Woody Allen, American filmmaker
Stanley Kubrick, American filmmaker
Mike Leigh, English filmmaker
Malcolm McDowell, English actor
Paul Newman, American actor and director

This section lists contemporaries whom the playwright may or may not have known.

Vanessa Redgrave, English actress

George Romero, American filmmaker

Francois Truffaut, French filmmaker

POLITICS/ MILITARY

Kofi Annan, Ghanaian UN Secretary General

Jacques Chirac, French president

Mikhail Gorbachev, Russian politician

Vaclav Havel, Czech writer and politician

John Hume, Northern Irish politician

Slobodan Milosevic, Serbian president; charged as a war criminal by the UN

Gloria Steinem, American feminist activist

Malcolm X, American activist

SCIENCE

Yuri Gagarin, Russian cosmonaut

Joseph L. Goldstein, American scientist

Jane Goodall, English zoologist

Stephen Hawking, English physicist

Brian David Josephson, Welsh physicist

John Forbes Nash Jr., American mathematician

Carl Sagan, American astronomer

Robert Wilson, American astronomer

LITERATURE

Isaac Asimov, Russian-American writer

Umberto Eco, Italian novelist

Dario Fo, Italian novelist

Joseph Heller, American novelist

John le Carré, English novelist

Thomas Pynchon, American novelist

Kurt Vonnegut, American novelist

Tom Wolfe, American author

RELIGION/ PHILOSOPHY

Michel Foucault, French philosopher
Jacques Derrida, French philosopher
Tenzin Gyatso, Tibetan Dalai Lama
Jean-François Lyotard, French philosopher
Robert Nozick, American philosopher
Pope Benedict XVI
Richard McKay Rorty, American philosopher
Bernard Williams, English philosopher

SPORTS

Henry Aaron, American baseball player
Muhammad Ali, American boxer and activist
Jim Brown, American football player
Phil Esposito, Canadian hockey player
Sandy Koufax, American baseball player
Willie Mays, American baseball player
Pele, Brazilian soccer player
Johnny Unitas, American football player

BUSINESS AND INDUSTRY

Warren Buffett, American investor
Lorne Michaels, Canadian television executive
Rupert Murdock, Australian media mogul
Ralph Nader, American consumer advocate
Carlos Slim, Mexican telecommunications businessman
Swraj Paul, Indian-British business magnate
Sir Alan Sugar, English entrepreneur
Donald Trump, American business magnate

STOPPARD

in an hour

PRESENT PERFECT TENSE

Tom Stoppard is, by all indications, not finished writing plays that are both important and popular. He has won major awards in each of the last four decades, demonstrating an uncanny ability to make arcane and/or dated subjects seem relevant, intriguing, and entertaining to contemporary audiences.

TURMOIL TO STABILITY

Tomas Straussler was born to Martha and Eugene Straussler on July 3, 1937, in Zln, Czechoslovakia. Eastern Europe was very unstable at this time, and to be a Jewish family greatly magnified the danger. In an attempt to avoid the influence of anti-Semitic measures, the Strausslers left Europe entirely and attempted to settle in the British sector of Singapore in 1939. The move provided only a short window of stability, as Japanese forces invaded in 1941. Martha and her children fled again, along with many British nationals, to Darjeeling,

---

This is the core of the book. The essay places the playwright in the context of his or her world and analyzes the influences and inspirations within that world.

India. Eugene chose to stay behind and fight, but the British forces fell to the Japanese. Eugene was captured and died in a prison camp.

Shortly after Eugene's death, Martha married British Army Major Kenneth Stoppard. Martha had begun to adopt British culture as her own, and chose not to disclose that she was fully Jewish. Martha was justifiably fearful of being singled out or ostracized within her adopted culture and also did not want to lose Kenneth, who was devoutly Protestant. Tom lived to his sixties before finding out that all four of his grandparents and both of his birth parents were Jewish. As a child, he had only known that one of his grandparents was Jewish. Adding to Tom's cultural mishmash was the fact that his family now spoke English as its primary language, and he was enrolled in Darjeeling Academy, a private school run by American Methodists. This was short-lived, however, as the Stoppard family moved to Derbyshire, England, after the war ended.

In less than a decade of life, Czech refugee Tomas Straussler had become Britton Tommy Stoppard, and attended a proper English academy in Nottinghamshire. Kenneth Stoppard was an inveterate Anglophile, and was very pleased that the family had been able to ascend to a traditional British lifestyle. And despite the blur of locales, languages, and nationalities Tom had been associated with in his young life, he took quickly to the idea of being British. He would later say: "I came here when I was eight, and I don't know why, I don't particularly wish to understand why, but I just seized England and it seized me." Kenneth likely had something to do with Tom's enthusiasm for his adopted land. Tom would, however, cite the turbulence of his childhood as being a likely subconscious influence in his consistent use of confusion among characters.

A LIMITED BRUSH WITH ACADEMIA

With the idea of helping him to become a proper Brit, Tom was enrolled in the Dolphin School in Nottinghamshire, a formal English boarding school. After finishing there, he entered the Pocklington

School in Yorkshire, a similar institution. Despite his romance with British culture, Tom claimed that the overall influence of school was negative. He was critical of some of his instructors as well as feeling "bored and alienated by everyone from Shakespeare to Dickens besides." Tom left school early, claiming, somewhat ironically, to be "bored by the idea of anything intellectual." He completed O-Levels in Greek and Latin prior to leaving school. Stoppard never received a university education, choosing instead to move back in with his mother and stepfather. He found work as a journalist for the *Western Daily Press* in Bristol in 1954, and dreamt of being a hard-boiled, on-location reporter, sent to the most dangerous, war-torn areas. Like many of Stoppard's early interests and experiences, this desire made its way into his work at a much later date.

THE THEATER BUG

In 1958, Stoppard expanded his journalistic repertoire, writing as both a humorist and theater critic. Mostly, he reviewed plays put on by the Bristol Old Vic Repertory. He claims that viewing the 1958 production of *Hamlet*, with Peter O'Toole in the title role, was a defining moment for him. Indeed he was willing to pass off review assignments to other reviewers in order to view subsequent performances. Stoppard began to spend his social time with young actors such as O'Toole, and he was known for being awkward amongst his theater friendship circle. Also, his status as an admittedly second-tier reviewer gave him something to prove, and he was attracted to the way playwrights were revered. He decided that his future was as a playwright. However, he did not begin actually writing plays at this point.

After a few years of simply thinking about writing, Stoppard decided to set his plan to action. While on holiday in 1960, he came to the conclusion that he would never begin writing dramatic works if he did not start immediately. So he quit his columnist job to ensure he would have the proper motivation. He wrote his first dramatic work, *A Walk on the Water*, and within a week of submission was contacted by the well-known agent Kenneth Ewing. While *A Walk on the Water* was not put into production quickly, the simple contact from the agent was considered a major event in Stoppard's career by the playwright. However, he needed work, so he applied to a British theater magazine called *Scene*. And he was back to reviewing plays. The catch was that the magazine did not pay its writers, so Stoppard borrowed money from Ewing as well as other friends. And he developed a habit of living outside his means, frequently resulting in his being broke. *A Walk on the Water* was eventually sold to British TV, and Stoppard was paid £350, with which he financed a ten-week Mediterranean vacation with his then girlfriend, Isabelle Dunjohn. Naturally, this resulted in Stoppard returning with no money, and he set back to work on new plays.

SUCCESS IN LIMBO

A Walk on the Water was, by Stoppard's admission, a play that borrowed liberally from Robert Bolt's *Flowering Cherry* and Arthur Miller's *Death of a Salesman*. This was, however, a very common trend among fledgling British writers. Despite the spate of similar competition, in 1963 the television network that picked it up planned on making it the "play of the week." But, ultimately, this was derailed by the Kennedy assassination, and the work aired with little fanfare. This naturally irritated Stoppard, as his potential big break would have to wait. Eventually, the teleplay would be revamped into *Enter a Free Man*, and it was performed on stage in 1968. The story centered on an inventor, George, his chimerical visions of what could be, and how his unrealistic visions hurt the stability of his family. Simplistic and predictable, the play follows George through his epiphanies and their subsequent failures to materialize. Eventually, the family reunites, though in a resigned fashion.

Ewing continued to shop Stoppard's work throughout the early 1960s, but *A Walk on the Water* remained the only play that sold. During a conversation regarding the O'Toole production of *Hamlet*,

Ewing suggested the idea of a play centering on Rosencrantz and Guildenstern. Stoppard immediately ran with the idea, deciding to have the duo run into a mad King Lear. The idea was parlayed into Stoppard being granted a five-month residency in a Berlin mansion in 1964. During that time, he penned a verse one-act entitled *Rosencrantz and Guildenstern Meet King Lear.*

He had left his new girlfriend, Jose Ingle, in England to do so. And he felt a bit caught between his professional and personal obligations. He had also been contracted to write a novel, and he felt that both tasks would best be accomplished away from Jose. In the end, he returned to Jose earlier than planned.

Stoppard revised his *Rosencrantz and Guildenstern* script. Its two-act prose version was optioned by the Royal Shakespeare Company, which asked for a third act. What seemed like a major breakthrough went for naught, as Stoppard's three-act version was returned to him without performance or further-development commission. Tom and Jose were married during this time. Jose had also become pregnant, making the rejection of the play a larger blow to the frequently destitute Stoppard.

Ewing finally found a venue for the fledgling work, the Edinburgh Fringe Festival. This was neither the venue nor scale the playwright or his agent were hoping for. Also, this meant that undergraduate actors instead of professionals would perform the play. However, despite low production levels (Stoppard referred to the stage as being the size of a Ping-Pong table), the play was raved about by numerous sources. It was then optioned by the National Theatre. Unfortunately, the option stipend was only for £50, and there was no guarantee that the play would ultimately see production. Jose gave birth to the couple's first son, Oliver, during this time of uncertainty, and the future of the Stoppard family seemed to be riding on countless variables.

Thankfully for Stoppard, a previously scheduled production of *As You Like It* was cancelled, and *Rosencrantz and Guildenstern Are Dead* premiered at the Old Vic Theatre. While it was a tortuous route to a successful premier, Stoppard became the youngest playwright to be staged through the National Theatre. The accolades began piling up, and it was clear that the struggle for success was over. When asked what he intended to accomplish with the play, Stoppard was quoted as saying that he wished for the play to make him very rich.

THE ANATOMY OF A HIT

The play drew inevitable comparisons to Samuel Beckett's *Waiting for Godot* and, to a lesser degree, Luigi Pirandello's *Six Characters in Search of an Author*. While the reviews were favorable as a whole, most of the negative articles called the play derivative for its similarities to Beckett and Pirandello. Stoppard's willingness to both reference and borrow from existing text, made him something of a puzzle to critics. While he was undoubtedly clever, it was common to downplay the importance of his work. Stoppard's play was pop, after all, and far more accessible than those works by more arcane existentialist writers.

Waiting for Godot and *Rosencrantz and Guildenstern Are Dead* share a number of common traits. They both use existentialist philosophies for humor and tragedy. Each has two main characters with similar speech patterns. Repetitive banter between the main characters is used throughout *Godot*, and frequently in *Rosencrantz and Guildenstern*. For example, both plays allow their main characters to observe others in a way that speaks to their own existential crises. In *Godot*, Vladimir and Estragon meet a beaten and tied-up wraith named Lucky and examine him as though he's not conscious, Vladimir deeming aspects of his state "not certain" and Estragon referring to the same things as "inevitable." When Rosencrantz and Guildenstern happen upon Hamlet, they have a similar discussion with the Player regarding Hamlet's sanity.

However, the stark aesthetics produce drastically different results. In Beckett's scene, the introduction of Lucky is an alienating and dis-comforting touch. The stark and blunt examination is both humanistic and nihilistic, due to the ambiguity of observations such as "It's inevitable." In Stoppard's work, however, the use of the fictional Hamlet makes such observations fanciful, playful, and engaging rather than alienating to the audience; Hamlet's condition is ultimately deemed "stark raving sane." The characters in *Rosencrantz and Guildenstern Are Dead* glean their own triviality, and the comic strength of the play comes from the willingness of the characters to creatively explore their circumstances while the audience enjoys the ride. This is in sharp contrast to Beckett; Vladimir and Estragon's perpetual staidness provides such an enormous level of alienation that the humor is inherently defensive.

While Beckett's play could be considered a jarring social commentary in a time of Western political stability (albeit in the wake of World War II), Stoppard wrote a play with little relevance during a time of considerable political change. This was also a source of criticism, as some reviewers tempered their praise by indicting Stoppard's lack of social commentary. Stoppard responded to this by saying: "I must stop compromising my plays with this whiff of social application. They must be entirely untouched by any suspicion of usefulness. I should have the courage of my lack of convictions." Stoppard's responses to criticisms often smack of a pithy curtness. At this point in his career, this brashness made Stoppard a bit of a rebel, as reviews could often make a significant difference in the revenue of plays. After all, Stoppard was only in the process of establishing his name. Most in his place would have either played it safe or declined to comment.

ABSURDITY AND REALITY

Criticisms aside, *Rosencrantz and Guildenstern Are Dead* immediately made Stoppard both a known and desirable name. He remained active in the theater in the following years, focusing on overseeing the first major production of *Enter a Free Man* and introducing several one-acts.

The most prominent of these works was *The Real Inspector Hound* (1968). It was a farcical one-act play-within-a-play. It had a notable, or perhaps notorious, distinction when it opened. A long-running Agatha Christie play, *The Mousetrap*, was playing at the same time in the same area of London. The Stoppard play was a transparent derision of the staple conventions of British parlor whodunits such as *The Mousetrap*. There was the potential for contention on the basis of the plot element, but this was not the primary concern of the Christie production. The idea that there was a "real" Inspector Hound (as opposed to an impostor) was a summation of the climatic plot twist in *The Mousetrap*. This not only infuriated those involved in *The Mousetrap*, but it also kept them from being able to publicly comment without drawing direct attention to the surprise ending of their own production.

The play also lampooned the theater critic, Stoppard's previous profession. The two critics in the play are both caricatures. One is obsessed with personal advancement, and the other with using his status to woo actresses. The name "Birdboot" was likely an allusion to William Boot, Stoppard's pseudonym when he wrote as a theater critic. Both critics in the play write bombastic reviews before eventually becoming involved in the "play" itself. They both reminisce about the "Old Vic," where *Rosencrantz and Guildenstern Are Dead* premiered and where Stoppard reviewed plays, and Stoppard may have been directly mocking particular critics, as the play certainly does not paint theater critics in a positive light. Stoppard considered himself to be a lower-stature critic, asked to review plays of lesser prominence than his peers. At the end of *The Real Inspector Hound*, three critics of greater stature lie dead, the last one by the hand of the character who is ultimately revealed as the lowest-ranking critic.

Another inclusion in the script was the philandering Birdboot's description of his boredom and disappointment in marriage. The absurd nature of *The Real Inspector Hound* keeps Birdboot's laments from seeming to be a direct indictment of Stoppard's personal situation. But there is a moment where Birdboot receives a call from his wife, on the stage of the play-within-a-play. He goes through an exasperated defense before giving his wife saccharin platitudes and hanging up. Friends of Stoppard described him as being more focused on family life than anything else. But, by many accounts, Jose had been adversely affected by her husband's success, and Stoppard's home life was not stable.

Stylistically, *The Real Inspector Hound* starts with plot-driving elements of the whodunit and play-within-a-play. In the second half, when the critics Birdboot and Moon are unwittingly made part of the whodunit, it uses touches of classical farce. These include mistaken identity and characters trading places. There is also a lot of repeated dialogue with different meanings. The absurd and farcical touches can be traced to Shakespeare's *A Comedy of Errors* and Ionesco's *The Bald Soprano*, among others. But as in *Rosencrantz and Guildenstern Are Dead*, it is not the components' originality that defines Stoppard's plays, it is the juxtaposition and execution.

The play also shared similarities with Oscar Wilde's *The Importance of Being Earnest*. This is true in the sense that the original source material (in Wilde's case, the classic romantic parlor drama à la Jane Austen) was being lampooned even though the play itself was faithful to and reliant on its conventions. This was certainly not the last of Stoppard's allusions to Wilde.

NOT EXEMPLARY

Stoppard's late 1960s–early 1970s foray into one-acts can be attributed to his worry about being labeled a one-hit wonder. It was also true that by this time his marriage was crumbling. Jose had suffered a nervous breakdown, and Tom began a romantic relationship with Dr. Miriam Moore-Robinson (later Stoppard). Jose gave birth to the couple's second son, Barnaby. But shortly after his birth, Stoppard sought and received outright custody of his two sons, one still an infant. He then moved in with Moore-Robinson, who raised the children as her own.

Tom later stated that to divorce with children of those young ages did not paint him as an exemplary father.

The divorce from Jose would not be finalized until 1972. But the move to live with Moore-Robinson began a comparatively lengthy period of familial stability. By the time the divorce was granted, Miriam was pregnant.

DELVING FURTHER INTO FARCE

While *The Real Inspector Hound* borrowed mostly from farce, *After Magritte* (1970) was a clear dip into absurdism. The short play borrows liberally from French absurdism. In particular, Stoppard's extensive stage directions utilize some Magritte-inspired props and visuals. The plot is simplistic. It revolves around an absurd argument between spouses. Ultimately a detective and policeman are involved.

Two years later, Stoppard wrote a radio play, *Artist Descending a Staircase* (1972), using Marcel Duchamp in a similar way to Magritte in *After Magritte*. The action of the play involves an absurd mystery. Stoppard also makes transparent references to Duchamp, including the character names — Martell and Beauchamp.

With these plays, Stoppard was in step with the growing resurgence of British farce, led by the late Joe Orton on stage and Monty Python on television. The mid-sixties to early seventies were marked by a growing number of comedic works that mocked traditional British sensibilities. *The Real Inspector Hound* and *After Magritte* both contain elements of this, though neither could be said to deride British life with the focus or intensity of a play such as Orton's *Entertaining Mr Sloan* (1964).

American theater was in a much different place at this time, as the Off-Broadway movement was giving rise to experimental theater. Groups like Richard Schechner's The Performance Group and Cafe La Mama performed work of playwrights such as Sam Shepard. This school of theater flatly avoided most facets of the modern American (or British) play. Instead, it focused more on ritual change, mythological themes, and radical politics. Stoppard would have numerous Off-Broadway productions, but he would not be relevant to this side of the Off-Broadway movement.

In 1971, Stoppard wrote *Dogg's Our Pet*. While it is best known in combination with *The 15-Minute Hamlet*, the non-*Hamlet* portion is based upon an idea introduced by philosopher Ludwig Wittgenstein in his book *Philosophical Investigations*. The play hinges on the idea that two parties are speaking different languages, with common lexicons. They are able to communicate with one another without realizing that different languages are being spoken. On its own, the play was more of an application of the idea than a stand-alone dramatic work.

PUTTING THINGS BACK TOGETHER, IN A SENSE

Tom and Miriam married in February of 1972, a month after his divorce was granted and a month before their first (Tom's third) child, William, was born. Tom dedicated *Jumpers* (1972) to Miriam. It was his first full-length play of the decade. *Jumpers* had numerous touches that referred back to the one-acts, such as a bizarre murder mystery and a detective attempting to make sense of a seemingly absurd circumstance. But it is a departure from earlier works in two ways. The dialogue is filled with lengthy speeches. There are also a kitchen sink of literary and philosophical references that push the plot and dialogue. The heaviness of both the references and the interminable speeches underpinned both the rave and the tepid reviews.

Jumpers won several major awards — but split audiences. Some people were swept up in the play throughout. Others lost patience with the lengthy speeches that broke up the action. The speeches are like George Bernard Shaw's in nature, but the plot elements certainly are not. Ultimately, it can be said that George, the main character, drives the play. He has an ongoing desire to make an argument for the philosophical absolute. There is an unsolved murder of an acrobat who happens to be George's primary rival. Marital enmity results from both ennui and accusations of pet murder. And Archie, a jack-of-all-trades, seems to be controlling the plot action even when not onstage.

Jumpers is easily Stoppard's most inaccessible play, both due to the sheer number of references and the diversity of the source material. The play furthers Stoppard's dialogue with Wittgenstein. It utilizes a dead body in a way similar to Joe Orton's *Loot*, and it muses intermittently on the then-recent phenomena of moon landings. George appears with shaving foam on his face, carrying a tortoise. The original cast featured recent Bond-girl and noted stage actress Diana Rigg in the role of Dotty, who is George's wife and a dethroned former musical-theater star. (Rigg's notoriety added to the in-joke layering of the play). Furthermore, the play opened at the Old Vic, giving it one more reference point to Stoppard's personal history. Balancing all of these references fits with Stoppard's gymnastic theme of the play. Stoppard attempts the very difficult task of using intensely visual staged action, while at the same time engaging in dense, lengthy speeches. George's musings are certainly clever, but they require a tremendous audience attention span. During the non-monologue portions, the contentiousness between and observations of George and Dotty provide many of the plays stronger moments, despite a lack of gravitas in their exchanges.

Unlike previous plays (and many of those to come), the attempts of characters to understand their surroundings are not limited to any classifiable circumstance or setting. While Rosencrantz and Guildenstern exist within a plot known to the audience, George looks for absolutes within human consciousness. But he also can be called to comment on unusual, digressive goings-on. For example, he frequently carries a tortoise, but laments his inability to find his hare. Dotty is also frequently in stages of undress, and the play is the first of Stoppard's to utilize sexual tension. The inclusion of such a wide variety of plot points, and the verbose orations resulting can be seen as the greatest strength or weakness of *Jumpers*. The sheer breadth of the language often forces the somewhat farcical plot to the backseat, again, drawing opposing reactions, such as these when the play was revived recently on Broadway:

> The trouble is that this three-level prestidigitation never achieves the desired interrelation. We get instead more or less cleverly excogitated, linguistically acrobatic flippancy, along with characters who bypass the heart and end up not mattering. — John Simon, *New York Magazine*

> And a play often dismissed as too clever by half now registers clearly as a poignant acknowledgement of the limits of cleverness. — Ben Brantley, *The New York Times*

Despite the descent into a coda at the end (a scene that has changed multiple times in revisions) and general strangeness in the plot, Stoppard referred to the play as an "absolutely traditional straight" play about "people who don't know very much about what's going on." Stoppard despised naturalism, and critics categorizing his elaborately absurd play as such was a stab at the austere posterity he felt naturalism embodied. "I think that sort of truth-telling writing is as big a lie as the deliberate fantasies I construct. It's based on the fallacy of naturalism. There's a direct line of descent which leads you down to the dregs of bad theatre, bad thinking, and bad feeling." Certainly, no one would mistake *Jumpers* for naturalism, and it ends in a way that begs certain questions. Act Two ends with George finding his hare dead and stepping on his tortoise amidst a twisting scene that could hardly be described as denouement.

The self-awareness of the ending is another point of contention between those who find the play great and those who do not. The muddiness of the plot can be seen as the ultimate unraveling of George's archaic Logical Positivist view, because the lack of certainty did not keep the plot from unfolding and did not keep the play from ending. Others saw the muddiness of the plot as being simply muddy.

Ultimately, however, the disparate critical views and the sheer level of thought present in *Jumpers* make it a play that will continue to be discussed actively in a manner that few thirty-seven-year-old plays will.

BACK TO BASICS

The Stoppards moved to a large Victorian estate shortly after their marriage, and Miriam began a career as a television personality. Despite the *Jumpers* opening, Stoppard spent as much time as possible with his family. He relished the opportunity to be part of an idyllic, high-class British family. His writing also seemed to benefit. He was ready to release another full-length play two years later. *Travesties* (1974) was a contained, referential work. It drew far more from *Rosencrantz and Guildenstern Are Dead* than from *Jumpers* or the absurdist one-acts. *Travesties* confines its dramatic action to vitriolic arguments among historical figures. Meanwhile those same figures mime scenes from *The Importance of Being Earnest*. The impetus of this play was historical. The lead character, Henry Carr, did actually perform in a production of Wilde's play that was put on by James Joyce in Zurich. In addition to this, Dadaist Tristan Tzara and Vladimir Lenin were in Zurich at a similar (though not exactly identical) time. The play is a memory play, seen through the eyes of an elder Henry Carr. It features very stark exchanges of sociopolitical jargon inspired by actual works or beliefs of Lenin and Tzara. It uses poetic games, such as speaking in limericks, and dialogue appropriated (with circumstantial changes) from *The Importance of Being Earnest*.

While *Travesties* does not have the sprawling plot of *Jumpers*, it does feature lengthy speeches. Most wordy digressions are historical chronologies. Future productions often shortened certain parts, most notably Cecily's Lenin lecture at the beginning of Act Two. The historical speeches provide a great deal of context for the historical characters. It's a good idea to become familiar with *The Importance of Being Earnest* before watching the play, as the digressions into the Wilde play are easily recognizable. While some take entire exchanges nearly verbatim, others use a Wilde "hook" and build off of it.

Wilde:

ALGERNON: All women become like their mothers. That is their tragedy. No man does. That's his.

JACK: Is that clever?

ALGERNON: It is perfectly phrased! and quite as true as any observation in civilized life should be.

JACK: I am sick to death of cleverness. Everybody is clever nowadays. You can't go anywhere without meeting clever people. The thing has become an absolute public nuisance. I wish to goodness we had a few fools left.

ALGERNON: We have.

JACK: I should extremely like to meet them. What do they talk about?

ALGERNON: The fools? Oh, the clever people, of course.

JACK: What fools.

Stoppard:

CARR: How illogical, since the war itself had causes. I forget what they were, but it was all in the papers at the time. Something about brave little Belgium, wasn't it?

TZARA: Was it? I thought it was Serbia . . .

CARR: Brave little Serbia . . . ? No, I don't think so. The newspapers would never have risked calling the British public to arms without a proper regard for succinct alliteration.

TZARA: Oh, what nonsense you talk!

CARR: It may be nonsense, but at least it is clever nonsense.

TZARA: I am sick of cleverness. The clever people try to impose a design on the world and when it goes calamitously

wrong they call it fate. In point of fact, everything is
Chance, including design.

CARR: That sounds awfully clever. What does it mean, not
that it has to mean anything, of course.

TZARA: It means, my dear Henry, that the causes we know
everything about depend on causes we know very little
about, which depend on causes we know absolutely nothing about. And it is the duty of the artist to jeer and howl
and belch at the delusion that infinite generations of real
effect can be inferred from the gross expression of appar-
ent cause.

Exchanges like this are the strength of *Travesties*, and many other
Stoppard works. The reference is a jumping-off point and serves to be
a familiar inlet, making the entire exchange more accessible and
multifaceted. Similar tactics have been used in pieces as disparate as
Richard Schechner's *Dionysus in '69* (1970) and David Henry Hwang's
M. Butterfly (1988).

Travesties ends abruptly. In the midst of Carr having an argument
with Joyce (a factually based argument, as the two sued one another in
real life), the final pairing off of *The Importance of Being Earnest* usurps
the scene. Carr (as Algernon) and Tzara (as Jack) unite with Cecily and
Gwendolyn, respectively. Immediately after this, Cecily and Carr
become old, completing the memory. Meanwhile Cecily, pokes factual
holes in Carr's story. Carr is not terribly thrown by this; instead he
waxes rhapsodic on the amazingly complex and confusing time that he
had in Zurich. This musing leads the audience back to the nonsensical
first minutes of the play, which featured exclamations in Russian,
Dadaist "chance" musings, and repeated English non-sequiturs. The
circular progression is a clear allusion to Joyce's structure, and further
unites the play with its own references. This also marked the first time
Stoppard worked with director Peter Wood. Stoppard would work
with Wood throughout the coming decades.

FEMALE CHARACTERS TO DATE

By the mid-seventies, Miriam Stoppard had made a name for herself as a radio/television host, advice columnist, and author. Her primary focus was women's and children's health. For Tom, female characters were usually either absent or used more as plot devices. *Travesties* marked the first presence of a pedantic female character in a Stoppard play. However, the characters of Cecily and Gwendolyn, both Wilde namesakes, could not be said to be purely Stoppard creations.

Dirty Linen (1976) was written during the first wave of Feminism. Like much of Stoppard's work to date, the play used British conventions, but it was iconoclastic to a popular movement. The onstage action is close to a Benny Hill sketch. The lone female character is frequently in states of undress amongst (supposedly secretly) lascivious men. The male characters are all House of Commons members, and the names of the characters and unseen dinner locations are excessively suggestive. The woman, Maddie Gotobed, has been made Secretary, despite her lack of qualifications. She is treated (transparently) the way a group of patriarchal philanderers would treat a beautiful but unintelligent woman.

The intended morality of the play is questionable. Was the play simply a response to the Women's Movement, in the way it provided a farce that was so deeply entrenched in double entendre and tawdriness that the potentially offensive action loses meaning? Was the play more of a satire of the British sense of propriety, meaning Maddie (and the frequent appearance of loose undergarments) is more representative of the actual practices of British people, despite the roundabout attempts to cover up the prevailing sexual revolution? Certainly, the scandal-obsessed media is also a subject, as the papers are printing a report that one woman, revealed later to be Maddie, has accused 119 members of the House of impropriety. But Maddie's own stated stance is in sharp contrast to the media's insistence that she has been taken advantage of.

All in all, the play is a departure from Stoppard's earlier work. It stands out as being more simplistic and formulaic than his other plays.

Some of the licentious dialogue resembles that of Joe Orton, but, unlike in Orton, the plot stays very one-dimensional.

> CHAMBERLAIN: What?! — that luscious creature is our clerk! Impossible! Where's her moustache? Her dandruff? Her striped pants?
>
> *(Maddie reflexively slams her knickers drawer.)*
>
> What an uncommonly comely clerk you are! My name's Douglas. I hope you don't mind me saying that you're a lovely girl! — I don't mind telling you that if I wasn't married to a wonderful girl myself with two fine youngsters down in Dorking and an au pair to complicate my life, I'd be after you and no mistake . . .

Stoppard was inspired to add *New-Found-Land* (1976) to *Dirty Linen* when Ed Berman, his frequent director, become a British citizen. Berman was an American beforehand, and the short play becomes a laundry list of American clichés. The characters of *Dirty Linen* exit the room, and the two *New-Found-Land* players enter, only to be interrupted and replaced by the *Dirty Linen* characters after the description of America concludes.

FINALLY, POLITICS!

Despite brushes with politics in a historical sense in *Travesties* and in a mocking tone in *Dirty Linen*, Stoppard had not yet treated politics as a primary subject. This changed after he began getting personally involved. Stoppard became associated with Amnesty International. He was interested in meeting political dissidents from Eastern Europe. During 1977, he met Russian dissident Vladimir Bukovsky and Czech dissident Vaclav Havel. Havel would become president of Czechoslovakia and, subsequently, the Czech Republic. Bukovsky briefly campaigned to become a 2008 Russian presidential candidate, but he was not allowed to run.

These meetings engendered what would become Stoppard's primary political focus: the rejection of oppressive governments. Stoppard's Czech origin and Havel's profession as a playwright led Stoppard to be a key player in getting Havel's plays translated to English. The meeting with Bukovsky and other exiled Russians led to *Every Good Boy Deserves Favour* (1977), Stoppard's first openly political play.

Every Good Boy Deserves Favour was written at the request of Viktor Fainberg. It is partially based on the real-life experience of Bukovsky. The play is very short, and requires a full orchestra, making it difficult to perform. In the play, the KGB will not allow a political prisoner, Ivanov, to go free unless he admits to psychological deficiencies that caused him to oppose the government. The orchestra is a fantasy of Ivanov's cellmate, a schizophrenic, who believes an orchestra is within his control. Meanwhile, the teacher of Ivanov's son, a clear mouthpiece for the state, informs the boy that his father's condition is both legitimate and severe.

Bukovsky was one of the first prominent figures to speak out publicly against the Soviet Union's usage of psychiatric prisons. He was arrested after publishing a document of his personal experiences. Western pressure led to the release (and exile) of many dissidents (including Bukovsky) in the seventies. However, the Iron Curtain of Eastern European communism was still very strong, and this became a focus of many of Stoppard's subsequent plays.

Night and Day sticks out as well. The play was certainly relevant to the time. The fictional African country's leader, Mageeba, is a clear allusion to Idi Amin. It lacks much of the playfulness in language and circumstances that can be found in most of Stoppard's other plays. *Night and Day* features mostly realistic dialogue (the character of Ruth has an audible inner monologue), and the characters are pragmatically proactive instead of impetuous or contemplative.

The other characters are made up of two reporters, a photographer, a mining magnate, his wife, their child, and their servant. The ongoing question throughout the play revolves around the paradox of the press being at once a service, a means to profit, and a way to shape ideas. While the characters all have their own ideas on the matter, nobody seems to give a strong point of view. Wagner, the grizzled union man, and Milne, the young idealist, are natural rivals. While it seems that Stoppard identifies more with the young Milne, who is ultimately martyred for what turns out to be no real purpose, his favorable treatment of Milne can be traced to Milne's desire to remain truly independent. He does not present a clear and preferable grand-scale alternative to the existing media quagmire. *Night and Day* was the culmination of Stoppard's early desire to be in the profession and the position that many of the characters were in. The death of Milne could ultimately be seen as Stoppard's own romanticism with the press being laid to rest.

The character of Ruth, with her audible inner monologue, is a somewhat odd inclusion in the play. She vacillates between being an unfulfilled wife with a wandering eye for journalists and the play's moral compass. Her lack of vested interest allows her to speak about the political and media situation at hand. She had an affair with Wagner in the past, and she has a fantasy about Milne during the play, but her sexual side seems misplaced. This issue is not limited to Ruth, however. The primary difficulty within the play is determining whose story it is, or at least finding a cohesive way to view the play in its entirety. The dialogue is far more on-the-nose than in other Stoppard plays. For the first time, it can be said that Stoppard was more interested in storytelling than in fanciful creation. The strength of the play is in what the characters are going to say or do, rather than in how they say or do it. Even Ruth's monologues report goings-on. One familiar with Stoppard's earlier plays might suspect that such a device would be used to tie in some kind of outside context, but that is not the case here. In the encounter with Mageeba, Ruth's inner monologue says the "truth" about her feelings. However, given the circumstances, these feelings could be deduced without being "spoken."

("RUTH" is the notation for the audible inner monologue.)

MAGEEBA: You see, I know everything. I am like the father to all citizens of Kambawe. In your case, of course, that would be difficult to imagine.
RUTH: Of course.
"RUTH": Wrong!
MAGEEBA: Such is our legacy of racial and cultural prejudice.
RUTH: Yes, indeed.
"RUTH": *(Loudly.)* Geoffrey!!

All in all, *Night and Day* is probably Stoppard's least regarded major play, and ironically it seems digressive from his work due to its simplicity.

Dogg's Hamlet, Cahoot's Macbeth (1979) is the combination of *Dogg's Our Pet*, *The 15-Minute Hamlet*, and *Cahoot's Macbeth*. The overall effect is the type of political play that one would, in contrast with *Night and Day*, very much expect from Stoppard. The Wittgenstein influence in the language of "*Dogg*" is juxtaposed with the presence of an Inspector in *Cahoot's Macbeth*. The play has some aesthetic and topical similarities to Vaclav Havel's *The Memorandum* (1965). The biggest difference between the two works is that the nonsense language in *The Memorandum* is a tool of bureaucratic oppression, while the "*Dogg*" language (the alternate word meanings) becomes a refuge from the Inspector's inquiries. Heavily truncated versions of *Hamlet* and *Macbeth* are present, but they are used in very different ways. *Dogg's Hamlet* presents the entire story uninterrupted, while *Cahoot's Macbeth* breaks up the Shakespeare plot, and the play-within-the-play becomes both a framing device and an impetus for the Inspector's inquisitions.

The plot of *Cahoot's Macbeth* fits nicely within Stoppard's works, but the play was inspired by actual events. Czech playwright Pavel

Kahout did indeed stage an underground production of *Macbeth*, and he was the subject of government persecution. Further, the Inspector refers to the actor playing *Macbeth* as "Landovsky," after Pavel Landovsky, an actor in Kahout's troupe. Theater players who were arrested in Czechoslovakia were not allowed to perform on commercial stages, and Kahout referred to his production group as LRT — Living Room Theatre.

Cahoot's Macbeth, especially within historical context, showcases Stoppard's ability to juxtapose. He is both a comedic and a menacing character. The Inspector seems to be literate in theater, but his name dropping suggest that he studies plays and actors the way law enforcement agents study fugitives. Using phrases such as "any Tom, Dick, or Bertolt," and criticizing the performance amidst threats, the Inspector is one of Stoppard's most dominant presences. His early exchanges are reminiscent of the theatrical tradition of exposing the destructive absurdity of power, a theme found in virtually every era.

When looked at as one work, *Dogg's Hamlet, Cahoot's Macbeth* blends disparate concepts yet the overall work is oddly cohesive. In his forward, Stoppard succinctly states: "The first is hardly a play without the second, which cannot be performed without the first."

The late seventies also saw a resurgence of the Conservative movement in Britain, with Margaret Thatcher becoming prime minister when the Tory Party came to power. Stoppard admits to voting for Thatcher's party, but not identifying with all tenets of it, calling himself a "conservative with a little 'c.'" Thatcher was not popular with most artists and playwrights. Stoppard's politics are best defined as being anti–large government, and pro–civil liberties.

A SLEW OF ADAPTATIONS

Stoppard's foray into translations and adaptations began in 1979, and the next decade saw him focus primarily on the works of nineteenth- and early-twentieth-century Eastern European playwrights. *Undiscovered Country* (1979) and *Dalliance* (1986) were both based on

Arthur Schnitzler plays, *Das weite Land* and *Liebelei*, respectively. Both were noted for being more comic than the originals; however, Stoppard still made note that each was an "English version" of the Schnitzler work. His hope was to use his name to draw attention to these plays and playwrights, rather than to receive credit for his own adaptations.

On the Razzle (1981) was definitely an adaptation, however. Stoppard was not the first to adapt the source material. Thorton Wilder had already adapted the source play, Johann Nestroy's *Einen Jux will er sich machen*, twice. Wilder's second adaptation, *The Matchmaker*, had been adapted yet again into *Hello, Dolly*. Stoppard's version was very much a classical farce, making frequent use of malapropisms, double entendres, and mistaken identities. Stoppard's quick dialogue complements Nestroy's plot very well. While the play is one of his lesser-known works, it is still performed by community theaters and high schools, which can accommodate the need for a large cast. *On the Razzle* is different from most Stoppard works due to its constant plot action, as well as the lack of any self-aware speeches by the characters.

Stoppard finds the play writing process very enjoyable, and has often said that the plot is the most difficult part for him to conceive. The existence of an involved plot in *On the Razzle* allowed him to focus on playful dialogue. The play follows a traditional farce pattern. Two workers decide to skip work and go out on the town, or "on the razzle," and immediately things become complicated. Weinberl and Christopher enter a clothing store. Weinberl, when informed that the cloak he is holding has been reserved by a woman, informs the clerk that he is the woman's husband — only to have the woman in question enter the store. As is the case with most light farces, the characters are reactive and go along with odd circumstances rather than question them.

MME KNORR: . . . I think it is so romantic — you must have
     swept her off her feet. Tell me, how long have you known
     each other?
MRS. FISCHER: Not long at all.
WEINBERL: No, not long.

MME KNORR: You must have been married with your head
in a whirl!

MRS. FISCHER: You couldn't say I went into it with my eyes
open.

MME KNORR: Of course you did, and I am sure you have
not been disappointed.

MRS. FISCHER: Surprised more than disappointed. My husband has a very individual way of dealing with the banal-
ities of ordinary time — I expect we'll be engaged next
week and exchanging cards the week after.

Ultimately, it is revealed that Weinberl and Mrs. Fischer were
previously exchanging love letters under pseudonyms, and the elabo-
rate ruse turns into romance, as do the rest of the play's misunder-
standings.

On the Razzle featured Felicity Kendal in a "trouser role" as
Christopher. Kendal would become a fixture both in Stoppard's plays
and in his personal life.

THINGS GET PERSONAL

If politics is considered the first common theatrical subject that
Stoppard conspicuously avoided and then embraced it, romance was the
second. Many earlier plays had marital relationships and lustful characters but ignored the characters' emotions, focusing instead on intellectual rationalizations. This all changed in *The Real Thing* (1982). The
play was dedicated to Miriam, and, like *Night and Day*, it did not seem
to fit within Stoppard's works-to-date. Unlike *Night and Day*, *The Real
Thing* was very positively received. It had a Broadway run of sixteen
months, more than double the length of any of Stoppard's previous or
subsequent plays.

The male lead in *The Real Thing* was Henry, a playwright,
Stoppard's first transparent self-reference. Unlike previous characters
with relevance to Stoppard's life, there is no tongue-in-cheek playful-

ness to Henry. He deals with emotion in a straightforward and visceral way, something that cannot be said about any of Stoppard's earlier characters. The play has moments very similar to Harold Pinter's *Betrayal* (1978). However, Pinter's characters maintain an absolute if superficial composure throughout, while Stoppard's characters are openly vulnerable, giving the plays two entirely different effects. While there are no direct references or previous source material for *The Real Thing*, it features dialogue that is stylistically close to other plays, particularly on the subject of infidelity.

> HENRY: Yes. Did you?
> ANNIE: No.
> HENRY: Did you want to?
> ANNIE: Oh, for God's sake!
> HENRY: You can ask me.
> ANNIE: I prefer to respect your privacy.

At this juncture, characters like those in *Betrayal* or others with tactful "modern" British sensibilities would change the subject. Stoppard does not.

> HENRY: I have none. I disclaim it. Did you?
> ANNIE: What about your dignity, then?
> HENRY: Yes, you'd behave better than me. I don't believe in behaving well. I don't believe in debonair relationships. "How's your lover today, Amanda?" "In the pink, Charles. How's yours?" I believe in mess, tears, pain, self-abasement, loss of self-respect, nakedness. Not caring doesn't seem much different from not loving. Did you? You did, didn't you?

Henry's rejection of stoicism is similar to Stoppard's own rejection of naturalism. At this time, there was an increasing trend in popular culture for characters to acknowledge, accept, or even embrace infidelity as something to be expected in modern life. Henry's willingness to make things ugly and messy can be seen as Stoppard's own response to this trend.

Henry also functions as an avatar for Stoppard's views on playwriting; however, Henry's focus is far more on the negative critical side than anything else. Annie (Henry's wife) has a pet cause in a political prisoner, Brodie, and she gives Henry a manuscript that Brodie wrote. Henry's response affords Stoppard an opportunity to speak through his character, and Stoppard decided to send Henry in armed with a cricket bat.

HENRY: Shut up and listen. This thing here, which looks like a wooden club, is actually several pieces of particular wood cunningly put together in a certain way so that the whole thing is sprung, like a dance floor. It's for hitting cricket balls with. If you get it right, the cricket ball will travel two hundred yards in four seconds, and all you've done is give it a knock like knocking the top off a bottle of stout, and it makes a noise like a trout taking a fly . . . (*He clicks his tongue to make the noise.*) What we're trying to do is to write cricket bats, so that when we throw up an idea and give it a little knock, it might . . . *travel* . . . (*He clicks his tongue again and picks up the script.*) Now, what we've got here is a lump of wood roughly the same shape trying to be a cricket bat, and if you hit the ball with it, the ball will travel about ten feet and you will drop the bat and dance about shouting "Ouch!" with your hands stuck into your armpits. (*Indicating the cricket bat.*) This isn't better because somebody says it's better, or because there's a conspiracy by the MCC to keep cudgels off the field. It's better because it's better. You don't believe me, so I suggest you go out to bat with this and see how you get on. "You're a strange boy, Billy, how old are you?" "Twenty, but I've lived more than you'll ever live." Ooh, ouch!

(He drops the script and hops about with his hands in his armpits, going "Ouch!" ANNIE watches him expressionlessly until he desists.)

The cricket-bat diatribe, in conjunction with multiple assertions that Henry is an outstanding writer, points to Stoppard's own ego about his writing. Yet there is also a self-effacing facet present in *The Real Thing*. Henry is interested in pop music, not classical or opera. While a minor point of the plot, it fits with the criticism of Stoppard's canon. Despite the intellectual topics present in many of Stoppard's plays, critics have regularly cited Stoppard's work as lacking substance, much as a music critic might characterize pop music. Henry works to try to understand classical music, even going so far as to find plagiarism in Bach, but, ultimately, the play ends with Henry choosing to listen to The Monkees.

No other Stoppard play would have nearly the personal relevance as had *The Real Thing*. Furthermore, life imitated art nearly a decade later. Felicity Kendal was the original Annie in London (Glenn Close played the role in the first Broadway production), and the play's plot saw Henry and Annie, playwright and actress, leaving their spouses for one another. This would be eerily similar to real-life events in the early 1990s.

MATH LESSONS

In 1988, Stoppard went back to intellectual source material, only this time he went with physics. *Hapgood* differed from any Stoppard work in genre and plot, but it bore recognizable Stoppard touches in its treatment of Cold War politics and in the creativity of applying scitntific properties to characters.

Hapgood is, simply put, a twisting play about espionage during the Cold War. Its plot appears to be heavily influenced by the novels of John Le Carré, more so than those of Robert Ludlum or Ian Fleming. Like much of Le Carré, the action is centered on human interaction rather than on larger, "doomsday"-themed possibilities. The play, however, spends a lot of time dawdling over characters' possible allegiances, "real" versus "fake" documents, and cryptic "spy-speak" dialogue. The play's critical reception was tepid. Most reviews posited that the lengthy mathematical analogies took away from the tortuous spy story, or vice versa.

Hapgood was Stoppard's first full-length play with a female lead, and, naturally, Felicity Kendal played Hapgood. The play begins with a botched briefcase exchange, and immediately loyalties are questioned. The logical suspect is a Russian double agent named Kerner, who is also revealed to be the father of Hapgood's son. As in many spy thrillers, the "romance" elements are cursory, and while Hapgood and Kerner speak of love, there is little passion in the script. Kerner is repeatedly referred to as "ours" or "theirs" by other characters in reference to allegiance. And although Kerner does not double-cross his British comrades, when offered a choice between life with Hapgood and their son he chooses to return to the Soviet Union, a decision demonstrating that he was ultimately "theirs."

The duplicitous analogies are pervasive throughout *Hapgood*, and they are frequently translated to mathematical philosophies. Kerner is the translator, as questions of his alliances or those of the botched delivery yield mathematical answers. Kerner posits that twins are the cause of the ensuing perfidy; when asked to expound, he responds:

KERNER: The particle world is the dream world of the intelligence officer. An electron can choose to be here or there in the same moment. You can choose. It can go from here to there without going in between; it can pass through two doors at the same time, or from one door to another in a path which is there for all to see until someone looks, and then the act of looking has made it take a different path. Its movements cannot be anticipated because it has no reasons. It defeats surveillance because when you know what it's doing you can't be certain where it is, and when you know where it is, you can't be certain what it's doing: Heisenberg's uncertainty principle; and this is not because you're not looking carefully enough, it is because there is *no such thing* as an electron with a definite position and a definite momentum; you fix one, you lose the other, and it's all done without tricks, it's the real world, it is awake.

HAPGOOD: Joseph, please explain to me about the twins.

KERNER: I did but you just missed it.

The rest of the action can all be tied to this speech, as the exposed villain, Ridley, does have a twin, and Hapgood acts as though she has a twin to snare Ridley (and his twin). Hapgood can only act erratically as her twin, and thus her "twin" becomes the electron. The denouement, however, demonstrates the limitations of the analogy, as Kerner cannot both return to Russia and stay with Hapgood.

LIFE AND ART INTERTWINE

While there was certainly speculation that Tom Stoppard and Felicity Kendal had more than a professional relationship, the suspicions were not publicly confirmed until late 1990, when the British tabloid press began seeing the two out in public regularly. Both were still technically married, but they had probably been separated from their spouses by then, especially Kendal, whose divorce became final in early 1991. Stoppard's divorce became final in early 1992. Kendal had also been born in India. Stoppard wrote a radio play, *In the Native State*, about the relationship between the Anglo and native cultures prior to India's independence. He dedicated it to Kendal, and it showed a considerably more multifaceted point of view than Stoppard's customary "good vs. bad" political approach. Kendal was also a muse for *Shakespeare in Love* (which Stoppard was writing at this time). Stoppard used little details, such as the female romantic lead playing a male role (as Kendal did in *On The Razzle*), that seemed directly tied to his romance with

Kendal. All in all, his relationship with Kendal opened up a new side to his work, one of a more gentle romantic nature.

MATH LESSONS, PART II

Arcadia (1993) premiered five years after *Hapgood*, and again the plot featured a large mathematical presence. *Arcadia* is one of Stoppard's most highly regarded plays, primarily because the richness of the references work very well within the plot. The different themes are also complementary, and the play does not feel forced or intellectual for the sake of being intellectual.

Arcadia is very much an ensemble piece, and it has two major story lines. One begins in 1809 and one in 1989; both are set in a British manor. The 1809 sections focus mostly on Thomasina, a teenage mathematical savant, and Septimus, her tutor. Thomasina understands mathematical concepts beyond both her years and her time, but she is far more interested in understanding and experiencing romantic emotions. Her affection is directed toward Septimus, who is involved in a scandalous affair of his own.

The twentieth-century section is dominated by an intellectual quorum, each cast member focused on different elements of the history of the manor. The group is often contentious, mostly due to the brashness of Bernard and his desire to engage Hannah. The different theories of the members are at times corroborated or contradicted by the 1809 characters acting out the events in scenes that overlap those of the contemporary group.

The primary mathematical basis of the play is the second law of thermodynamics, having to do with entropy. Entropy, scientifically, describes decay, as its figurative use would suggest, but its applications span from the dissipation of energy leading to the inevitable end of stars (or anything else that gives off energy), to the disorder of chaos theory, and both of these meanings are thematically present in *Arcadia*. Thomasina sees love as both chaotic and consumptive, and her untimely demise is the result of a fire, the literal application of the mathematical property. The modern-day group tries to figure out the identity of a hermit who is revealed to have followed a mathematical calculation for countless years, a reference to the infinite iterations of chaos theory.

The headiness of the source material does not undermine the entertainment value of the dialogue. Unlike *Night and Day* and *Hapgood*, Stoppard's dialogue in *Arcadia* has no forced affectations, and the potentially digressive forays into historical or mathematical topics further the plot rather than simply provide context. If one play could best demonstrate Stoppard's strengths as a playwright, *Arcadia* would be the logical choice. The opening minutes efficiently manage to be humorous, to introduce intellectual context, and to provide several plot points.

> THOMASINA: Septimus, what is carnal embrace?
> SEPTIMUS: Carnal embrace is the practice of throwing one's arms around a side of beef.
> THOMASINA: Is that all?
> SEPTIMUS: No . . . a shoulder of mutton, a haunch of venison well hugged, an embrace of grouse . . . *caro, carnis*; feminine; flesh.
> THOMASINA: Is it a sin?
> SEPTIMUS: Not necessarily, my lady, but when carnal embrace is sinful, it is a sin of the flesh, QED. We had *caro* in our Gallic Wars — "The Britons live on milk and meat" — "*lacte et carne vivant*." I am sorry that the seed fell on the stony ground.
> THOMASINA: That was the sin of Onan, wasn't it, Septimus?
> SEPTIMUS: Yes, he was giving his brother's wife a Latin lesson and she was hardly the wiser after it than before. I thought you were finding a proof for Fermat's last theorem.
> THOMASINA: It is very difficult, Septimus. You will have to show me how.

SEPTIMUS: If I knew how, there would be no need to ask *you*. Fermat's last theorem has kept people busy for a hundred and fifty years, and I hoped it would keep *you* busy long enough for me to read Mr. Chater's poem in praise of love with only the distractions of its own absurdities.

THOMASINA: Our Mr. Chater has written a poem?

SEPTIMUS: He believes he has written a poem, yes. I can see that there might be more carnality in your algebra than in Mr. Chater's "Couch of Eros."

THOMASINA: Oh, it was not my algebra. I heard Jellaby telling cook that Mrs. Chater was discovered in carnal embrace in the gazebo.

SEPTIMUS: (*Pause.*) Really? With whom, did Jellaby happen to say?

(*Thomasina considers this with a puzzled frown.*)

THOMASINA: What do you mean, with whom?

SEPTIMUS: With what? Exactly so. The idea is absurd. Where did the story come from?

Economical dialogue could certainly not be considered a trademark of Stoppard, but even at a run time of three hours or so, *Arcadia* manages to be constantly moving, and the humor avoids heaviness. The plot is complex, but fluid. Most criticisms of the play were tempered by concessions to the skillfulness of Stoppard's integration of so many subjects, and mainly commented that the play could not effectively deliver on that many fronts. However, there was a greater sentiment that the play delivered on enough, if not all fronts.

HOUSMAN IN LOVE

The late 1990s saw production of two notable works with *Love* in the title, the play *The Invention of Love* and the film *Shakespeare in Love*. The similarity, however, ended with the titles and the use of a historical figure as a main character. Still, both works won multiple major awards. And while *Shakespeare in Love* was very popular, *The Invention of Love* is routinely considered Stoppard's most underrated, if not greatest play.

The play is reminiscent of *Travesties* in its blending of historical fact and fictionalized encounters in a memory-play format. And the River Styx setting gives it a license to shift freely. However, *Travesties* had a much lighter and more superficial feel, and its ending essentially trivializes the staged events. *The Invention of Love* is much more like *Arcadia*. In both, learning and emotion are abound, and while learning is the natural course for both Housman in *The Invention of Love* and Thomasina in *Arcadia*, both long to experience emotion — Thomasina openly, Housman more internally. Philology (the study of the interplay between literature and linguistics) is central to the play. While the plot itself is very sparse, the digressive musings of the characters over translations and meaning make up the spine of the play far more than the actual "events" do. This avoids the plot-vs.-speech confusion of *Jumpers*, and it allows Stoppard the freedom to delve into his subject without restraint.

Stoppard's arcane indulgences often split critics, but *The Invention of Love* was very well received, and most saw the light plot as necessary as opposed to problematic. The play ran for nearly a year in London, but its Broadway run lasted only three months, from March to June 2001. Audiences, particularly American audiences, had a lot of difficulty dealing with the esoteric references. The New York producers went so far as to hand out a thirty-page booklets of historical background to attendees.

The other prominent subject in the play is Housman's homosexuality, and his unrequited love for his friend, Moses Jackson. Housman is frequently caught up in the debate about the homosexual (and sometimes pederastic) lives of the philosophers and writers he studies. He is concerned about how their thoughts are valued by British society, but now their actions would be condemned. This naturally parallels Oscar Wilde's philosophy. In fact, Wilde and Housman have a dialogue toward the end of the play. Wilde's reference to himself as "Monsiour Melmoth," his self-given exile name after his prison term, as well as his general bitterness, in contrast to Housman's deference, present both a logical juxtaposition and the play's greatest question: Was it better for Housman to internalize his desires, only expressing them through verse, and to live a private and eventually solitary life, and to die old and respected? Or was it better for someone like Wilde to indulge his desires, become notorious, and eventually die young and poor, as a result of society's condemnation of his actions? The play does not have a timeless moral spin on homosexuality, only a time-specific societal one. On the late 1990s plays about homosexual issues were becoming increasingly common and popular. *Rent* won the 1996 Pulitzer, and *Love! Valor! Compassion!* beat out *Arcadia* for the Tony Award in 1995. Though it would not be logical to group *The Invention of Love* with these plays, it is worth noting that Stoppard's first prominent usage of homosexual themes came at a time when they were in vogue.

CLOSING THE DOOR

Right around the time *Shakespeare in Love* was premiering, Kendal and Stoppard broke up. As throughout Stoppard's career, personal turmoil coincided with a gap in major theatrical productions. Also, Stoppard's foray into plays centered on love seemed to end (if his work up to the present is any indication). In 1999 he announced that he was research-ing pre-revolution Russian artists for a new play.

BACK TO POLITICS . . . A LONG WAY BACK

After a five-year theatrical hiatus, Stoppard returned with an epic tril-ogy, *The Coast of Utopia*. The trilogy spans 1833 to 1868, and mostly centers on Alexander Herzen. But it also features a great deal of mate-rial on Michael Bakunin and other Russian historical figures. The play is huge, running nine hours on stage and requiring forty-two actors in its New York production. It first ran in repertory, the premieres of each part staggered by about a month, with the first part, *Voyage*, premiering in November of 2006, and all plays closing in May of 2007. It also won more Tony awards than any non-musical ever had. The play marked the first "straight" historical effort by Stoppard, in the sense that the story is a dramatization of the truthful historical story, without any creative juxtaposition (other than some time jumps in *Voyage*).

Herzen is a very interesting figure for Stoppard to focus on. Herzen is typically lumped in with other pre-communist revolutionaries. He has been overshadowed both by those who were involved in the actual revolution (decades after Herzen's death), and by novelists and poets of the era. In his 2007 foreword, Stoppard refers to Herzen as "my hero," certainly an odd statement from someone so outspokenly anti-communist. However, Herzen's revolutionary politics were not communist, and his distaste for the stratification of 1840s Russia did not lead him to wish for the exact opposite. Rather, the despotic rule of Nicholas I was Herzen's primary target. His fear was that Russia would trade one totalitarian, censoring government for another. Stoppard makes sure to include lines indicating Herzen's distaste for those who embodied the type of absolutist philosophy espoused by twentieth-century communist revolutionaries.

Herzen seems to be Stoppard's pet cause. While the play does not contain any transparent allusions to present day politics, the stance of Herzen — a thoughtful, revolutionary centrist — seems to fit Stoppard's own (mostly unspoken) political leanings. On the other side is Bakunin, the mercurial anarchist, who is both intriguing and frustrating to Herzen, but who remains his friend throughout.

The Coast of Utopia consists of the three plays, *Voyage*, *Shipwreck*, and *Salvage*, that do work together. But *Voyage*, outside of its abrupt end, seems to be the most accomplished play on its own. Herzen is a lesser figure in *Voyage*, but he is basically the protagonist of the other two plays. Stoppard makes sure to have Herzen present his opinion on virtually anything of great theoretical importance, as well as to allow him to regularly trump others in speeches.

From *Shipwreck*:

SAZONOV: *(Emotionally.)* We were children of the Decembrists. *(To Herzen.)* When you were arrested, by some miracle they overlooked me and Ketscher.

HERZEN: This is not a sensible conversation. There will have to be a European revolution first, and there's no sign of it. The opposition has no faith in itself. Six months ago meeting Ledru-Rollin or Louis Blanc in a café felt like being a cadet talking to veterans. Their superior condescension to a Russian seemed only proper. What had we to offer? Belinsky's articles and Granovsky's lectures on history. But these celebrities of the left spend their time writing tomorrow's headlines and hoping that someone else will make the news go with them. And don't they know what's good for us! Virtue by decree. They're building prisons out of the stones of the Bastille. There's no country in the world that has shed more blood for liberty and understands it less.

Somehow, this does make dramatic sense, as the play's complexity comes from the factional myopia of thought present in the historical time, and using Herzen (or any one character) as the barometer gives the play its direction and message. Without a clear agent, the play could easily come off as detached pronouncements. The Herzen-centric filter was not without protest, however. Stoppard and Ethan Hawke, the Broadway Bakunin, had a lengthy conversation about the fact that Bakunin never wins an argument against Herzen. This led to Stoppard giving Bakunin the last word in an early *Salvage* scene.

Stoppard's goal may have been to present a sufficient tribute to an underrepresented historical figure, but *The Coast of Utopia* became a theatrical event. The only problem may be that the play requires such a mammoth cast that it may not get many performances in the future.

ONE MORE LOOK BACK

While the *Coast of Utopia* has an epic, and reflective tone, *Rock 'n' Roll* (2006) has an earnest quality that incorporates the emotions present in idealism as much as the ideals themselves. Stoppard's foreword states that the primary inspiration was an argument between Milan Kundera and Valclav Havel regarding the Soviet occupation of Czechoslovakia. Stoppard's principal political themes still radiate throughout *Rock 'n' Roll*. As in *Cahoot's Macbeth*, the underground art (in this case, music) of dissidents is factually based.

And as in *The Real Thing*, the protagonist is relevant to Stoppard himself. Only in this case, the character of Jan is the "what if" version of Stoppard. Jan, unlike Stoppard, went to university, chose to return to Czechoslovakia, and became involved in dissent. Also, the use of music is prevalent. It represents the only insouciance available as the characters become increasingly entangled in politics. The play shifts back and forth in time. It ends with a Rolling Stones concert, based on a 1990 event facilitated by Vaclav Havel. While the political upheaval had its fallout, the ending is triumphant, and the older characters seem to reconnect with their idealism.

Stoppard's political statement with both *The Coast of Utopia* and *Rock 'n' Roll* is about the beauty and limits of idealism. Stoppard has referred to himself as a "timid Libertarian," and this can be seen in these plays. He clearly trusts individuals more than governments. He also opposes the belief that extremes are the only possible alternatives.

AN EARLY CONCLUSION

As a playwright, Stoppard is both playful and thoughtful, both serious and absurd, and both faithful and irreverent. His legacy is one of innovation and impressive diversity. His inspiration often stems from established material, but his inventiveness sets him apart from his predecessors and contemporaries. In a popular culture that increasingly relies on remakes, retreads, and retooling, it is hard not to marvel at what Stoppard has consistently accomplished. Using a known story to draw an audience, Stoppard has made the tired fashionable, the arcane accessible, and the plodding fun. The greatest testament to Stoppard may be the fact that the shifting artistic landscape has led to works that use known commodities becoming more in vogue than ever, but no one is marveling at the quality. Current writers appropriating Stoppard's creative juxtapositions would be a perfect way to add artistry to this trend, but it has not happened. It stands to reason that Stoppard's ability is not so much underused as it is rare.

DRAMATIC MOMENTS

from the Major Plays

On the Razzle (1981)
from Act One   40

The Real Thing (1982)
from Act Two, Scene 5   49

Arcadia (1993)
from Act One, Scene 1   58

These short excerpts are from the playwright's major plays. They give a taste of the work of the playwright. Each has a short introduction in brackets that helps the reader understand the context of the excerpt. The excerpts, which are in chronological order, illustrate the main themes mentioned in the In an Hour essay.

from **On the Razzle** (1981)
from Act One

CHARACTERS

    Zangler

    Marie

    Sonders

    Foreigner

    Gertrud

    Melchior

    Hupfer

[Zangler has previously voiced his desire to keep Sonders away from his niece, Marie.]

> *Zangler's Shop. The shop is closed. Weinberl and Christopher are absent. Sonders, half hidden, has sent the canister. Zangler is on to him.*

ZANGLER: Sonders!

MARIE: Uncle!

SONDERS: Herr Zangler!

ZANGLER: Unhand my foot, sir!

SONDERS: I love your niece!

ZANGLER: *(Outraged.)* My knees, sir? *(Mollified.)* Oh, my *niece. (Outraged.)* Well, my niece and I are not to be prised apart so easily, and nor are hers, I hope I make my meaning clear?

SONDERS: Marie must be mine!

ZANGLER: Never! She is a star out of thy firmament, Sonders! I am a Zangler, provision merchant to the beau-monde, top board for the Cheesemongers and number three on the Small Bore Club.

SONDERS: Only three?

ZANGLER: Do you suppose I'd let my Airedale be hounded up hill and — my heiress be mounted up hill and bank by a truffle-hound — be trifled with and hounded by a mountebank?! Not for all the tea in China! Well, I might for all the tea in China, or the rice — no, that's ridiculous — the preserved ginger then — no, let's say half the tea, the ginger, a shipment of shark-fin soup double-discounted just to take it off your hands —

SONDERS: All you think about is money!

ZANGLER: All I think about *is* money! As far as I'm concerned any man who interferes with my Marie might as well have his hand in my till!

SONDERS: I make no secret of the fact that I am not the *eminence grise* of Oriental trade, but I have expectations, and no outstanding debts.

(A man, a foreigner, visible in the street, starts knocking on the ship door. Marie has emerged from her cage and goes to deal with it.)

FOREIGNER: Grus Grott! *(He enters and shakes hands all round.)*

ZANGLER: We're closed for lunch. What expectations?

FOREIGNER: Enshuldigen!

ZANGLER: Closed!

FOREIGNER: Mein heren! Ich nicht ein customer . . .

ZANGLER: What did he say?

MARIE: I don't know, Uncle, I think he's a foreigner.

FOREIGNER: Gut morgen — geshstattensie — bitte shorn — danke shorn . . .

ZANGLER: We're closed! Open two o'clock!

FOREIGNER: Ich comen looken finden Herr Sonders.

ZANGLER: Here! Sonders!

FOREIGNER: Herr Sonders?

ZANGLER: No, *there* Sonders.

FOREIGNER: Herr Sonders? Ich haben ein document.

ZANGLER: He's a creditor!

FOREIGNER: Herr Sonders?

ZANGLER: No debts, eh?

FOREIGNER: Ja — dett! –

SONDERS: Nein, nein, I'm busy. Comen backen in the morgen.

(Sonders ushers the foreigner out of the shop. The foreigner is in fact a legal messenger who has come from Belgium to announce the death of Sonders' rich aunt. He succeeds in this endeavor at the end of the play.)

ZANGLER: I thought you said you had no debts!

SONDERS: No outstanding debts — run-of-the-mill debts I may have. I probably overlooked my hatter, who is a bit short. But as for my expectations, Herr Zangler, I have the honour to inform you that I have a rich aunt in Brussels.

ZANGLER: A rich aunt in Brussels! I reel, I totter, I am routed from the field! A rich aunt in Brussels — I'm standing here with my buttons undone and he has a rich aunt in Brussels.

SONDERS: She's going to leave me all her money.

ZANGLER: When is that?

SONDERS: When she's dead, of course.

ZANGLER: Listen, I know Brussels. Your auntie will be sitting up in bed in a lace cap when Belgium produces a composer.

SONDERS: I hope so because while she lives I know she'll make me a liberal allowance.

ZANGLER: A liberal allowance?! How much is that in Brussels? I'm afraid I'll never do business on the basis of grandiloquent coinage, and in the lexicon of the false prospectus "a liberal allowance" is the alpha and of my God, how many times do I have to tell you? — I will not allow my ward to go off and marry abroad.

SONDERS: Then stay I'll here and marry her, if that's your wont.

ZANGLER: And meanwhile in Brussels your inheritance will be eaten to the bone by codicils letting my wont wait upon her will like the poor cat with the haddock.

SONDERS: The what?

ZANGLER: Look to the aunt! Don't waste your time mooning and skulking around my emporium — I'm sending Marie away to a secret address where you will never find her, search how you will. *(To Gertud who has entered with Zangler's old uniform.)* What is it?!

GERTRUD: Twenty-three Carlstrasse, Miss Blumenblatt's.

SONDERS: Twenty-three Carlstrasse . . . ! Miss Blumenblatt's!

ZANGLER: *(Spluttering.)* You old — you stupid —

GERTRUD: Should I let Marie have the new travelling case?

ZANGLER: — old baggage!

GERTRUD: Not the new travelling case . . .

SONDERS: *(Leaving.)* My humble respects . . .

GERTRUD: Here is your old uniform. And the new servant has arrived.

SONDERS: Your servant, ma'am!

GERTRUD: His.

(Sonders goes.)

ZANGLER: You prattling old fool, who asked you to open your big mouth?

GERTRUD: You're upset. I can tell.

ZANGLER: Where is Marie?

GERTRUD: She's upstairs trying on her Scottish travelling outfit you got her cheap from your fancy.

ZANGLER: My fancy? My fiancée! A respectable widow and the Madame of "Madame Knorr's Fashion House."

GERTRUD: I thought as much — so it's a betrothal.

ZANGLER: No it isn't, damn your nerve, it's a hat and coat shop! Now get out and send in the new servant. And don't let Marie out of your sight. If she and Sonders exchange so much as a glance while I'm gone I'll put you on cabbage-water till you can pass it back into the soup-pot without knowing the difference.

(Exit Gertrud.)

ZANGLER: This place is beginning to lose its chic for me. I bestride the mercantile trade of this parish like a colossus, and run a bachelor establishment second to none as far as the eye can see, and I'm surrounded by village idiots and nincompetent poops of every stripe. It's an uphill struggle trying to instill a little tone into this place.

(There is a knock on the door.)

ZANGLER: Entrez!

(There is a knock on the door.)

ZANGLER: *(Furiously.)* Come in!

(Enter Melchior.)

MELCHIOR: Excuse me, are you the shopkeeper, my lord?

ZANGLER: You do me too much honour and not enough. I am Herr Zangler, purveyor of high-class provisions.

MELCHIOR: I understand you are in desperate need of a servant.

ZANGLER: You understand wrong. There's no shortage of rogues like you, only of masters like me to give them gainful employment.

MELCHIOR: That's classic. And very true. A good servant will keep for years, while masters like you are being ruined every day. How's business, by the way? — highly provisional, I trust?

ZANGLER: You strike me as rather impertinent.

MELCHIOR: I was just talking shop. Please disregard it as the inexperience of blushful youth, as the poet said.

ZANGLER: Do you have a reference?

MELCHIOR: No, I just read it somewhere.

ZANGLER: Have you got a testimonial?

MELCHIOR: *(Produces a tattered paper.)* I have, sir. And it's a classic, if I say so myself.

ZANGLER: Do you have any experience in the field of mixed merchandise?

MELCHIOR: Definitely, I'm always mixing it.

ZANGLER: Well, I must say, I have never seen a testimonial like it.

MELCHIOR: It's just a bit creased, that's all.

ZANGLER: "Honest, industrious, enterprising, intelligent, responsible, cheerful, imaginative, witty, well-spoken, modest, in a word classic . . ."

MELCHIOR: When do you want me to start?

ZANGLER: Just a moment, aren't you forgetting the interview?

MELCHIOR: So I am — how much are you paying?

ZANGLER: Six guilders a week, including laundry.

MELCHIOR: I don't do laundry.

ZANGLER: I mean the housekeeper will wash your shirts.

MELCHIOR: That's classic. I like to be clean.

ZANGLER: And board, of course.

MELCHIOR: Clean and bored.

ZANGLER: And lodging.

MELCHIOR: Clean and bored and lodging —

ZANGLER: All included.

MELCHIOR: Ah, board and lodging. How about sharing a bed?

ZANGLER: I won't countenance immorality.

MELCHIOR: Own bed. As for the board, at my last place it was groaning fit to bust, the neighbors used to bang on the walls.

ZANGLER: I assure you, no one goes hungry here: soup, beef, pudding, all the trimmings.

MELCHIOR: Classic. I always have coffee with my breakfast.

ZANGLER: It has never been custom here for the servant to have coffee.

MELCHIOR: You wouldn't want me to drink liquor from the stock.

ZANGLER: Certainly not.

MELCHIOR: I should prefer to avoid the temptation.

ZANGLER: I'm glad to hear it.

MELCHIOR: Agreed, then.

ZANGLER: What? Well, if you do a good job . . . coffee then.

MELCHIOR: From the pot?

ZANGLER: Ad liberandum.

MELCHIOR: Is that yes or no?

ZANGLER: Yes.

MELCHIOR: Sounds classic. Was there anything else you wanted me to ask me?

ZANGLER: No . . . I don't think so.

MELCHIOR: Well, that seems satisfactory. You won't regret this, sir —
    I have always parted with my employers on the best of terms.

ZANGLER: You have never been sacked?

MELCHIOR: Technically, yes, but only after I have let it be known by
    subtle neglect of my duties that the job has run its course.

ZANGLER: That's very considerate.

MELCHIOR: I don't like to cause offence by giving notice — in a ser-
    vant it looks presumptuous.

ZANGLER: That shows modesty.

MELCHIOR: Your humble servant, sir.

ZANGLER: Yes, all right.

MELCHIOR: Classic!

ZANGLER: Only you'll have to stop using that word. It's stupid.

MELCHIOR: There's nothing stupid about the word. It's just the way
    some people use it without discrimination.

ZANGLER: Do they?

MELCHIOR: Oh yes. It's absolutely classic. What are my duties?

ZANGLER: Your duties are the duties of a servant. To begin with you
    can make my old uniform look like new — and if that tailor shows
    his face tell him to go to hell.

*(Enter tailor, Hupfer. Hupfer brings with him Zangler's new uniform on
a tailor's dummy. The complete rig-out includes a ridiculous hat with
feathers, etc., polished riding boots with monstrous shining and very audible spurs, and the uniform itself, which is top heavy with gold buttons and
braid, etc. Leather strapping supports holsters for knife, gun, sword. The
general effect is sporting and musical. The new uniform is brighter than
the old, which is bright. The tailor is only responsible for the clothes. The
rest of the stuff is already in the room.)*

HUPFER: Here we are — the masterpiece is ready.

ZANGLER: You managed it, my dear Hupfer! In the nick of time.

MELCHIOR: Go to hell.

ZANGLER: Shut up!

MELCHIOR: *(To the dummy.)* Shut up!

HUPFER: Well, with the help of two journeymen tailors I have done the impossible — let me help you into it.

MELCHIOR: Too small.

HUPFER: *(Reacts to Melchior.)* I see you have a new servant, Herr Zangler.

ZANGLER: *(Cheerfully.)* Oh yes. I woke up this morning feeling like a new man. So I got one.

HUPFER: Trousers.

MELCHIOR: Too tight.

HUPFER: *(Wary distaste.)* He's a personal servant, is he?

ZANGLER: Yes, he is a bit, but I'd like to give youth a chance and then I like to kick it down the stairs if it doesn't watch its lip.

MELCHIOR: I worked for a tailor once. I cooked his goose for him.

HUPFER: There we are.

MELCHIOR: Everything went well until I got confused and goosed his cook.

ZANGLER: Pay attention. You may learn something.

MELCHIOR: After that he got a valet stand.

ZANGLER: You'll see how a trouser should fit . . . except it is a bit tight, isn't it?

(It is more than a bit tight.)

HUPFER: Snug.

ZANGLER: Snug? I'd be in trouble if I knelt down. I'm thinking of my nuptials.

HUPFER: It's the pressing.

ZANGLER: Exactly. I don't want them pressed.

HUPFER: Try the tunic.

ZANGLER: I like the frogging.

HUPFER: Can we please keep our minds on the tunic. Now let me help you.

ZANGLER: It's somewhat constricted, surely.

HUPFER: That's the style.

ZANGLER: But it's cutting me under the arms, the buttons will fly off if I sit down, and I can't breathe.

HUPFER: It's a uniform, it is not supposed to be a nightshirt.

ZANGLER: I don't understand it. You took my measurements.

MELCHIOR: Well, that explains it. If God had been a tailor there's be two and a half feet to the yard and the world would look like a three-cornered hat.

ZANGLER: And it's a day late.

MELCHIOR: And it would have been a day late. We'd all be on an eight-day week.

ZANGLER: Shut up.

MELCHIOR: *(To the dummy.)* Shut up.

ZANGLER: I suppose it will have to do, at a pinch. How do I look?

MELCHIOR: I'd rather not say.

ZANGLER: I order you — how do I look?

MELCHIOR: Classic.

ZANGLER: Shut up!

MELCHIOR: *(To Hupfer.)* Shut up!

HUPFER: You dare to let your servant speak to me like that?

MELCHIOR: In the livery of the Zanglers I am no man's minion.

ZANGLER: That's well said. What's your name?

MELCHIOR: Melchior.

ZANGLER: Melchior, throw this man out.

HUPFER: Don't touch me! You, sir, received your measurements from nature. The tailor's art is to interpret them to your best advantage, and move the buttons later. My humble respects. I will leave my bill.

MELCHIOR: *(Thrusting the dummy at Hupfer.)* Oh no you won't — you'll take him with you!

(Exit Hupfer.)

MELCHIOR: What should I do next?

****

from **THE REAL THING** (1982)
from Act Two, Scene 5

CHARACTERS

Annie

Henry

[Annie wants Henry to analyze the script that Brodie, her political prisoner and pet cause has given her. Henry is already tired of hearing about everything Brodie.]

ANNIE: Well?

HENRY: Oh — um — Strauss?

ANNIE: What?

HENRY: Not Strauss.

ANNIE: I meant the play.

HENRY: (*Indicating the script.*) Ah. The play.

ANNIE: (*Scornfully.*) *Strauss.* How can this be Strauss? It's in Italian.

HENRY: Is it? (*He listens.*) So it is.

Italian opera.

One of the Italian operas.

Verdi.

ANNIE: Which one?

HENRY: Giuseppe.

(*He judges from her expression that this is not the right answer.*)

Monty?

ANNIE: I mean which *opera*.

HENRY: Ah. (*Confidently.*) *Madame Butterfly*.

ANNIE: You're doing it on purpose.

(*She goes to the record player and stops it playing.*)

HENRY: I promise you.

ANNIE: You'd think that *something* would have sunk in after two years and a bit.

HENRY: I like it — I really do like it — quite, it's just that I can't tell them apart. Two years and a bit isn't very long when they're all going for the same sound. Actually, I've got a better ear than you — *you* can't tell the difference between the Everly Brothers and the Andrews Sisters.

ANNIE: There isn't any difference.

HENRY: Or we could split up. Can we have something decent on now?

ANNIE: No.

HENRY: All right. Put on one of your instrumental numbers. The big band sound. (*He does the opening of Beethoven's Fifth.*)

Da — da — da — *dah* . . .

ANNIE: Get *on*.

HENRY: Right.

(*He turns his attention to the script.*)

Stop me if anybody has said this before, but it's interesting how many of the all-time greats begin with B: Beethoven, the Big Bopper . . .

ANNIE: That's all they have in common.

HENRY: I wouldn't say that. They're both dead. The Big Bopper died in the same plane crash that killed Buddy Holly and Richie Valens, you know.

ANNIE: No, I didn't know. Have you given up the play or what?

HENRY: Buddy Holly was twenty-two. Think of what he might have gone on to achieve. I mean, if Beethoven had been killed in a plane crash at twenty-two, the history of music would have been very different. As would the history of aviation, of course.

ANNIE: *Henry*.

HENRY: The play.

(*He turns his attention back to the script.*)

ANNIE: How far have you got?

HENRY: Do you have a professional interest in this or is it merely personal?

ANNIE: Merely?

(Pause.)

HENRY: Do you have a personal interest or is it merely professional?

ANNIE: Which one are you dubious about?

(Pause.)

HENRY: Pause.

ANNIE: I could do her, couldn't I?

HENRY: Mary? Oh, sure — without make-up.

ANNIE: Well, then. *Three Sisters* is definitely off.

HENRY: Nothing's definite with that lot.

ANNIE: The other two are pregnant.

HENRY: Half a dozen new lines could take care of that.

ANNIE: If this script could be in a fit state, say, a month from now —

HENRY: Anyway, I thought you were committing incest in Glasgow.

ANNIE: I haven't said I'll do it.

HENRY: I think you should. It's classy stuff, Webster. I love all the Jacobean sex and violence.

ANNIE: It's Ford, not Webster. *And* it's Glasgow.

HENRY: Don't you work north of the West End, then?

ANNIE: I was thinking you might miss me — pardon my mistake.

HENRY: I was thinking you might like me to come with you — pardon mine.

ANNIE: You hadn't the faintest intention of coming to Glasgow for five weeks.

HENRY: That's true. I answered out of panic. Of course I'd miss you.

ANNIE: Also it *is* somewhat north.

(Henry 'shoots' her between the eyes with his forefinger.)

HENRY: Got you. Is it rehearsing in Glasgow?

ANNIE: (*Nods.*) After the first week. (*Indicating the script.*) Where've you got to?

HENRY: They're on the train.

'You're a strange boy, Billy. How old are you?'

'Twenty. But I've lived more than you'll ever live.'

Should I read out loud?

ANNIE: If you like.

HENRY: Give you the feel of it.

ANNIE: All right.

HENRY: I'll go back a bit . . . where they first meet. All right? (*Annie nods. Henry makes train noises. She is defensive, not quite certain whether he is being wicked or not.*)

(*Reading.*) 'Excuse me, is this seat taken?'

'No.'

'Mind if I sit down?'

'It's a free country.'

'Thank you.'

'(*He sits down opposite her. Mary carries on with reading her book.*)'

'Going far?'

'To London.'

'So, you were saying . . . So you think it's a free country.'

'Don't you?'

'This is it, we're all free to do as we're told.'

'My name's Bill, by the way. What's yours?'

'Mary.'

'I'm glad to make your acquaintance, Mary.'

'I'm glad to make yours, Bill.'

'Do you know what time this train is due to arrive in London?'

'At about half-past one, I believe, if it is on time.'

'You put me in mind of Mussolini, Mary.'

'Yes, you look just like him, you've got the same eyes.'

ANNIE: If you're not going to read it properly, don't bother.

HENRY: Sorry.

'At about half-past one, I believe, if it is on time.'

'You put me in mind of Mussolini, Mary. People used to say about Mussolini, he may be a Fascist, but at least the trains run on time. Makes you wonder why British Rail isn't totally on time, eh?'

'What do you mean?'

'I mean it's a funny thing. The Fascists are in charge but the trains are late often as not.'

'But this isn't a Fascist country.'

'Are you quite sure of that, Mary? Take the army — '

You're not going to do this, are you?

ANNIE: Why not?

HENRY: It's no good.

ANNIE: You mean it's not literary.

HENRY: It's not literary, and it's no good. He can't write.

ANNIE: You're a snob.

HENRY: I'm a snob, and he can't write.

ANNIE: I know it's raw, but he's got something to say.

HENRY: He's got something to say. It happens to be something extremely silly and bigoted. But leaving that aside, there is still the problem that he can't write. He can burn things down, but he can't write.

ANNIE: Give it back. I shouldn't have asked you.

HENRY: For God's sake, Annie, if it wasn't Brodie you'd never have got through it.

ANNIE: But it *is* Brodie. That's the point. Two and a half years ago he could hardly put six words together.

HENRY: He still can't.

ANNIE: You *pig*.

HENRY: I'm a pig, and he can't —

ANNIE: I'll smash you one. It's you who's bigoted. You're bigoted about what writing is supposed to be like. You judge everything as though everyone starts off from the same place, aiming at the same prize.

English Lit. Shakespeare out front by a mile, and the rest of the field strung out behind trying to close the gap. You all write for people who would like to write like you if they could only write. Well, screw you, and screw English Lit.!

HENRY: Right.

ANNIE: Brodie isn't writing to compete like you. He's writing to be heard.

HENRY: Right.

ANNIE: And he's done it on his own.

HENRY: Yes. Yes . . . I can see he's done a lot of reading.

ANNIE: You can't expect it to be English Lit.

HENRY: No.

ANNIE: He's a prisoner shouting over the wall.

HENRY: Quite. Yes, I see what you mean.

ANNIE: Oh shut up! I'd rather have your sarcasm.

HENRY: Why a play? Did you suggest it?

ANNIE: Not exactly.

HENRY: Why did you?

ANNIE: The committee, what's left of it, thought . . . I mean, people have got bored with Brodie. People get bored with anything after two or three years. The campaign needs . . .

HENRY: A shot in the arm?

ANNIE: No, it needs . . .

HENRY: A kick up the arse?

ANNIE: (*Flares.*) For Christ's sake, will you stop finishing my sentences for me!

HENRY: Sorry.

ANNIE: I've lost it now.

HENRY: The campaign needs . . .

ANNIE: A writer is harder to ignore. I thought, TV plays get talked about, make some impact. Get his case reopened. Do you think? I mean, Henry, what *do* you think?

HENRY: I think it makes a lot of sense.

ANNIE: No, what do you *really* think?

HENRY: Oh, *really* think. Well, I *really* think writing rotten plays is not in itself proof of rehabilitation. Still less of wrongful conviction. But even if it were, I think that anyone who thinks that they're bored with Brodie won't know what boredom is till they've sat through his apologia. Not that anyone will get the chance, because it's half as long as *Das Kapital* and only twice as funny. I also think you should know better.

ANNIE: You arrogant bastard.

HENRY: You swear too much.

ANNIE: Roger is willing to do it, in principle.

HENRY: What Roger? Oh *Roger*. Why the hell would Roger do it?

ANNIE: He's on the committee.

(Henry looks at the ceiling.)

It just needs a bit of work.

HENRY: You're all bent.

ANNIE: You're jealous.

HENRY: Of Brodie?

ANNIE: You're jealous of the idea of the writer. You want to keep it sacred, special, not something anybody can do. Some of us have it, some of us don't. *We* write, *you* get written about. What gets you about Brodie is he doesn't know his place. You say he can't write like a head waiter saying you can't come in here without a tie. Because he can't put words together. What's so good about putting words together?

HENRY: It's traditionally considered advantageous for a writer.

ANNIE: He's not a writer. He's a convict. *You're* a writer. You write *because* you're a writer. Even when you write *about* something, you have to think up something to write about just so you can keep writing. More well-chosen words nicely put together. So what? Why should that be *it*? Who says?

HENRY: Nobody says. It just works best.

ANNIE: Of *course* it works. You teach a lot of people what to expect from good writing, and you end up with a lot of people saying you write well. Then somebody who isn't in the game comes along, like Brodie, who really has something to write about, something real, and you can't get through it. Well, *he* couldn't get through *yours*, so where are you? To you, he can't write. To him, write is all you *can* do.

HENRY: Jesus, Annie, you're beginning to appal me. There's something scary about stupidity made coherent. I can deal with idiots, and I can deal with sensible argument, but I don't know how to deal with you. Where's my cricket bat?

ANNIE: Your cricket bat?

HENRY: Yes. It's my new approach.

(He heads out into the hall.)

ANNIE: Are you trying to be funny?

HENRY: No, I'm serious.

(He goes out while she watches in wary disbelief. He returns with an old cricket bat.)

ANNIE: You'd better not be.

HENRY: Right, you silly cow —

ANNIE: Don't you bloody dare —

HENRY: Shut up and listen. This thing here, which looks like a wooden club, is actually several pieces of particular wood cunningly put together in a certain way so that the whole thing is sprung, like a dance floor. It's for hitting cricket balls with. If you get it right, the cricket ball will travel two hundred yards in four seconds, and all you've done is give it a knock like knocking the top off a bottle of stout, and it makes a noise like a trout taking a fly . . . (*He clicks his tongue to make the noise.*) What we're trying to do is to write cricket bats, so that when we throw up an idea and give it a little knock, it might . . . *travel* . . . (*He clicks his tongue again and picks up the script.*) Now, what we've got here is a lump of wood roughly the same shape trying to be a cricket bat, and if you hit the ball with it, the ball will travel about ten feet and you will drop the bat and dance about shouting 'Ouch!' with your hands stuck into your armpits. (*Indicating the cricket bat.*) This isn't better because somebody says it's better, or because there's a conspiracy by the MCC to keep cudgels off the field. It's better because it's better. You don't believe me, so I suggest you go out to bat with this and see how you get on. 'You're a strange boy, Billy, how old are you?' 'Twenty, but I've lived more than you'll ever live.' Ooh, ouch!

(*He drops the script and hops about with his hands in his armpits, going 'Ouch!' Annie watches him expressionlessly until he desists.*)

****

from **ARCADIA** (1993)
from Act One, Scene 1

CHARACTERS

Thomasina
Septimus
Jellaby
Chater

[From early in Act One. Thomasina is Septimus' student. They are in the middle of a math lesson.]

THOMASINA: Septimus, what is carnal embrace?

SEPTIMUS: Carnal embrace is the practice of throwing one's arms around a side of beef.

THOMASINA: Is that all?

SEPTIMUS: No . . . a shoulder of mutton, a haunch of venison well hugged, an embrace of grouse . . . *caro, carnis*; feminine; flesh.

THOMASINA: Is it a sin?

SEPTIMUS: Not necessarily, my lady, but when carnal embrace is sinful, it is a sin of the flesh, QED. We had *caro* in our Gallic Wars— 'The Britons live on milk and meat'—'*lacte et carne vivant*'. I am sorry that the seed fell on the stony ground.

THOMASINA: That was the sin of Onan, wasn't it, Septimus?

SEPTIMUS: Yes, he was giving his brother's wife a Latin lesson and she was hardly the wiser after it than before. I thought you were finding a proof for Fermat's last theorem.

THOMASINA: It is very difficult, Septimus. You will have to show me how.

SEPTIMUS: If I knew how, there would be no need to ask *you*. Fermat's last theorem has kept people busy for a hundred and fifty years, and I hoped it would keep *you* busy long enough for me to read Mr

Chater's poem in praise of love with only the distractions of its own absurdities.

THOMASINA: Our Mr Chater has written a poem?

SEPTIMUS: He believes he has written a poem, yes. I can see that there might be more carnality in your algebra than in Mr Chater's 'Couch of Eros'.

THOMASINA: Oh, it was not my algebra. I heard Jellaby telling cook that Mrs Chater was discovered in carnal embrace in the gazebo.

SEPTIMUS: (*Pause.*) Really? With whom, did Jellaby happen to say?

(*Thomasina considers this with a puzzled frown.*)

THOMASINA: What do you mean, with whom?

SEPTIMUS: With what? Exactly so. The idea is absurd. Where did the story come from?

THOMASINA: Mr Noakes.

SEPTIMUS: Mr Noakes!

THOMASINA: Papa's landskip gardener. He was taking bearings in the garden when he saw — through his spyglass — Mrs Chater in the gazebo in carnal embrace.

SEPTIMUS: And do you mean to tell me that Mr Noakes told the butler?

THOMASINA: No. Mr Noakes told Mr Chater. *Jellaby* was told by the groom, who overheard Mr Noakes telling Mr Chater, in the stable yard.

SEPTIMUS: Mr Chater being engaged in closing the stable door.

THOMASINA: What do you mean, Septimus?

SEPTIMUS: So, thus far, the only people who know about this are Mr Noakes the landskip architect, the groom, the butler, the cook, and, of course, Mrs Chater's husband, the poet.

THOMASINA: And Arthur who was cleaning the silver, and the boot-boy. And now you.

SEPTIMUS: Of course. What else did he say?

THOMASINA: Mr Noakes?

SEPTIMUS: No, not Mr Noakes, Jellaby. You heard Jellaby telling the cook.

THOMASINA: Cook hushed him as soon as he started. Jellaby did not see that I was being allowed to finish yesterday's upstairs' rabbit pie before I came to my lesson. I think you have not been candid with me, Septimus. A gazebo is not, after all, a meat larder.

SEPTIMUS: I never said my definition was complete.

THOMASINA: Is carnal embrace kissing?

SEPTIMUS: Yes.

THOMASINA: And throwing one's arms around Mrs Chater?

SEPTIMUS: Yes. Now Fermat's last theorem—

THOMASINA: I thought as much. I hope you are ashamed.

SEPTIMUS: I, my lady?

THOMASINA: If *you* do not teach me the true meaning of things, who will?

SEPTIMUS: Ah. Yes, I am ashamed. Carnal embrace is sexual congress, which is the insertion of the male genital organ into the female genital organ for the purposes of recreation and pleasure. Fermat's last theorem, by contrast, asserts that when x, y, and z are whole numbers each raised to the power of n, the sum of the first two can never be equal to the third when n is greater than two.

(Pause.)

THOMASINA: Eurghhh!

SEPTIMUS: Nevertheless, that is the theorem.

THOMASINA: It is disgusting and incomprehensible. Now when I am grown to practise it myself I shall never do without thinking of you.

SEPTIMUS: Thank you very much, my lady. Was Mrs Chater down this morning?

THOMASINA: No. Tell me more about sexual congress.

SEPTIMUS: There is nothing more to be said about sexual congress.

THOMASINA: Is it the same as love?

SEPTIMUS: Oh no, it is much nicer than that. *(One of the side doors leads to the music room. It is on the other door which now opens to admit Jellaby, the butler.)*

I am teaching, Jellaby.

JELLABY: Beg your pardon, Mr Hodge, Mr Chater said it was urgent you receive his letter.

SEPTIMUS: Oh, very well. (SEPTIMUS *takes the letter.*) Thank you. (*And to dismiss Jellaby.*) Thank you.

JELLABY: (*Holding his ground.*) Mr Chater asked me to bring me your answer.

SEPTIMUS: My answer?

(He opens the letter. There is no envelope as such, but there is a 'cover' which, folded and sealed, does the same service. SEPTIMUS tosses the cover negligently aside and reads.)

Well, my answer is that as is my custom and my duty to his lordship I am engaged until a quarter to twelve in the education of his daughter. When I am done, and if Mr Chater is still there, I will be happy to wait upon him — (*He checks the letter.*) — in the gunroom.

JELLABY: I will tell him so, thank you, sir.

(SEPTIMUS folds the letter and places it between the pages of 'The Couch of Eros'.)

THOMASINA: What's for dinner, Jellaby?

JELLABY: Boiled ham and cabbages, my lady, and a rice pudding.

THOMASINA: Oh, goody.

(Jellaby leaves.)

SEPTIMUS: Well, so much for Mr Noakes. He puts himself forward as a gentleman, a philosopher of the picturesque, a visionary who can move mountains and cause lakes, but in the scheme of the garden he is as the serpent.

THOMASINA: When you stir your rice pudding, Septimus, the spoonful of jam spreads itself round making red trails like the picture of the meteor in my astrological atlas. But if you stir backward, the jam will not come together again. Indeed, the pudding does not notice and continues to turn pink just as before. Do you think that is odd?

SEPTIMUS: No.

THOMASINA: Well, I do. You cannot stir things apart.

SEPTIMUS: No more you can, time must needs run backward, and since it will not, we must stir our way onward mixing as we go, disorder out of disorder into disorder until pink is complete, unchanging and unchangeable, we are done with it for ever. This is known as free will or self-determination.

(He picks up the tortoise and moves it a few inches as though it had strayed, on top of some loose papers, and admonishes it.)

Sit!

THOMASINA: Septimus, do you think God is a Newtonian?

SEPTIMUS: An Etonian? Almost certainly, I'm afraid. We must ask your brother to make it his first enquiry.

THOMASINA: No, Septimus, a Newtonian. Septimus! Am I the first person to have thought of this?

SEPTIMUS: No.

THOMASINA: I have not said yet.

SEPTIMUS: 'If everything from the furthest planet to the smallest atom of our brains acts accordingly to Newton's law of motion, what becomes of free will?'

THOMASINA: No.

SEPTIMUS: God's will.

THOMASINA: No.

SEPTIMUS: Sin.

THOMASINA: *(Derisively.)* No!

SEPTIMUS: Very well.

THOMASINA: If you could stop every atom in its position and direction, and if your mind could comprehend all the actions thus suspended, then if you were really, *really*, good at algebra you could write the formula for all the future; and although nobody can be so clever as to do it, the formula must exist just as if one could.

SEPTIMUS: (*Pause.*) Yes. (*Pause.*) Yes, as far as I know, you are the first person to have thought of this. (*Pause. With an effort.*) In the margin of his copy of *Arithmetica*, Fermat wrote that he had discovered a wonderful proof of his theorem but, the margin being too narrow for his purpose, did not have room to write it down. The note was found after his death, and from that day to this —

THOMASINA: Oh! I see now! The answer is perfectly obvious.

SEPTIMUS: This time you may have overreached yourself.

(*The door is opened, somewhat violently. Chater enters.*)

Mr Chater! Perhaps my message miscarried. I will be at liberty at a quarter to twelve, if that is convenient.

CHATER: It is not convenient, sir. My business will not wait.

SEPTIMUS: Then I suppose you have Lord Croom's opinion that your business is more important than his daughter's lesson.

CHATER: I do not, but, if you like, I will ask his lordship to settle the point.

SEPTIMUS: (*Pause.*) My lady, take Fermat into the music room. There will be an extra spoonful of jam if you find his proof.

THOMASINA: There is no proof, Septimus. The thing that is perfectly obvious is that the note in the margin was a joke to make you all mad.

(*Thomasina leaves.*)

SEPTIMUS: Now, sir, what is this business that cannot wait.

CHATER: I think you know it, sir. You have insulted my wife.

SEPTIMUS: Insulted her? That would deny my nature, my conduct, and the admiration in which I hold Mrs Chater.

CHATER: I have heard of your admiration, sir! You insulted my wife in the gazebo yesterday evening!

SEPTIMUS: You are mistaken. I made love to your wife in the gazebo.

She asked me to meet her there, I have her note somewhere, I dare say I could find it for you, and if someone is putting it about that I did not turn up, by God, sir, it is a slander.

CHATER: You damned lecher! You would drag down a lady's reputation to make a refuge for your cowardice. It will not do! I am calling you out!

SEPTIMUS: Chater! Chater, Chater, Chater! My dear friend!

CHATER: You dare to call me that. I demand satisfaction!

SEPTIMUS: Mrs Chater demanded satisfaction and now you are demanding satisfaction. I cannot spend my time day and night satisfying the demands of the Chater family. As for your wife's reputation, it stands where is ever stood.

CHATER: You blackguard!

SEPTIMUS: I assure you. Mrs Chater is charming and spirited, with a pleasing voice and a dainty step, she is the epitome of all the qualities society applauds in her sex — and yet her chief renown is for a readiness that keeps her in a state of tropical humidity as would grow orchids in her drawers in January.

CHATER: Damn you, Hodge, I will not listen to this! Will you fight me or not?

SEPTIMUS: (*Definitively.*) Not! There are no more than two or three poets of the first rank now living, and I will not shoot one of them dead over a perpendicular poke in the gazebo with a woman whose reputation could not be adequately defended with a platoon of musketry deployed by rota.

CHATER: Ha! You say so! Who are the others? In your opinion? — no — no — ! — this goes very ill, Hodge. I will not be flattered out of my course. You say so, do you?

SEPTIMUS: I do. And I would say the same to Milton were he not already dead. Not the part about his wife, of course —

CHATER: But among the living? Mr Southey?

SEPTIMUS: Southey I would have shot on sight.

CHATER: (*Shaking his head sadly.*) Yes, he has fallen off. I admired 'Thalaba' *quite*, but 'Madoc', (*He chuckles.*) oh dear me! — but we are straying from business here — you took advantage of Mrs Chater, and if that were not bad enough, it appears every stableboy and scullery maid on the strength —

SEPTIMUS: Damn me! Have you not listened to a word I said?

CHATER: I have heard you, sir, and I will not deny I welcome your regard, God knows one is little appreciated if one stands outside the coterie of hacks and placemen who surround Jeffrey and the *Edinburgh* —

SEPTIMUS: My dear Chater, they judge a poet by the seating plan of Lord Holland's table!

CHATER: By heaven, you are right! And I would very much like to know the name of the scoundrel who slandered my verse drama 'The Maid of Turkey' in the *Piccadilly Recreation*, too!

SEPTIMUS: 'The Maid of Turkey'! I have it by my bedside! When I cannot sleep I take up 'The Maid of Turkey' like an old friend!

CHATER: (*Gratified.*) There you are! And the scoundrel wrote he would not give it to his dog for dinner were it covered in bread sauce and stuffed with chestnuts. When Mrs Chater read that, she wept, sir, and would not give herself to me for a fortnight — which recalls me to my purpose —

SEPTIMUS: The new poem, however, will make your name perpetual —

CHATER: Whether it do or not —

SEPTIMUS: It is not a question, sir. No coterie can oppose the acclamation of the reading public. 'The Couch of Eros' will take the town.

CHATER: Is that your estimation?

SEPTIMUS: It is my intent.

CHATER: It is, is it? Well, well! I do not understand you.

SEPTIMUS: You see I have an early copy — sent to me for review. I say review, but I speak of an extensive appreciation of your gifts and your rightful place in English literature.

CHATER: Well, I must say. That is certainly . . . You have written of it?

SEPTIMUS: (*Crisply.*) Not yet.

CHATER: Ah. And how long does . . . ?

SEPTIMUS: To be done right, it first requires a careful re-reading of your book, of both your books, several readings, together with outlying works for an exhibition of deference or disdain as the case merits. I make notes, of course, I order my thoughts, and finally, when all is ready and I am *calm in my mind* . . .

CHATER: (*Shrewdly.*) Did Mrs Chater know of this before she — before you —

SEPTIMUS: I think she very likely did.

CHATER: (*Triumphantly.*) There is nothing that woman would not do for me! Now you have an insight into her character. Yes, by God, she is a wife to me, sir!

SEPTIMUS: For that alone, I would not make her a widow.

CHATER: Captain Brice once made the same observation!

SEPTIMUS: Captain Brice did?

CHATER: Mr Hodge, allow me to inscribe your copy in happy anticipation. Lady Thomasina's pen will serve us.

SEPTIMUS: Your connection with Lord and Lady Croom you owe to your fighting her ladyship's brother?

CHATER: No! It was all nonsense, sir — a canard! But a fortunate mistake, sir. It brought me the patronage of a captain of His Majesty's Navy and the brother of a countess. I do not think Mr Walter Scott can say as much, and here I am, a respected guest at Sidley Park.

SEPTIMUS: Well, sir, you can say you have received satisfaction.

****

Stoppard

THE READING ROOM

YOUNG ACTORS AND THEIR TEACHERS

Notes on Drama: *Rosencrantz and Guildenstern Are Dead*. http://www.an
swers.com/topic/rosencrantz-guildenstern-are-dead (date and author
unknown) [Chicago 17:32-34]

SCHOLARS, STUDENTS, PROFESSORS

Edwards, Paul. Science in *Hapgood* and *Arcadia*. Taken from *The Cambridge Companion to Tom Stoppard*. Cambridge, UK: Cambridge University Press, 2001.

Levenson, Jill L. Stoppard's Shakespeare: textual re-visions. Taken from
The Cambridge Companion to Tom Stoppard. Cambridge, UK: Cambridge University Press, 2001.

Vanden Heuvel, Michael. "Is Postmodernism?": Stoppard among/against
the postmoderns. Taken from *The Cambridge Companion to Tom
Stoppard*. Cambridge, UK: Cambridge University Press, 2001.

Zeifman, Hersh. The Comedy of Eros: Stoppard in Love. Taken from *The
Cambridge Companion to Tom Stoppard*. Cambridge, UK: Cambridge
University Press, 2001.

THEATERS, PRODUCERS

Sommer, Elyse. An Overview of Tom Stoppard's Career. http://www.cur
tainup.com/stoppard.html (date unknown)

Tom Stoppard — Complete Guide to the Playwright's Plays.http://www.doo
llee.com/PlaywrightsS/stoppard-tom.html (author and date unknown)

This extensive bibliography lists books about the playwright according to whom the books might be of interest. If you would
like to research further something that interests you in the text, lists of references, sources cited, and editions used in this
book are found in this section.

ACTORS, DIRECTORS, THEATER PROFESSIONALS

Bull, John. Tom Stoppard and Politics. Taken from *The Cambridge Companion to Tom Stoppard*. Cambridge, UK: Cambridge University Press, 2001.

THE EDITIONS OF STOPPARD'S WORKS USED FOR THIS BOOK

Stoppard, Tom. *Arcadia*. London, England: Faber and Faber, 1993, second printing. [ISBN 0-571-16934-1]

_____. *The Coast of Utopia* [*Voyage, Shipwreck, Salvage*]. first edition. New York, N.Y.: Grove Press, 2003, [ISBN 10: 978-0-8021-4340-2, ISBN 13: 0-8021-4340-7]

_____. *Hapgood*. London, England: Faber and Faber, 1988, 1994 (with corrections). [ISBN 0-571-19857-0]

_____. *The Invention of Love*. New York, N.Y.: Grove Press, 1997. [ISBN 0-8021-3581-1]

_____. *Jumpers*. New York, N.Y.: Grove Press, 1972. [ISBN 0-8021-5100-0]

_____. *Plays 4* [*Dalliance, Undiscovered Country, Rough Crossing, On the Razzle, The Seagull*]. London, England: Faber and Faber, 1999. [ISBN 0-57119-750-7]

_____. *The Real Inspector Hound and Other Plays* [*The Real Inspector Hound, After Magritte, Dirty Linen, New-Found-Land, Dogg's Hamlet, Cahoot's Macbeth*]. New York, N.Y.: Grove Press, 1993. [ISBN 10: 978-0-8021-3561-2, ISBN 13: 0-8021-3561-7]

_____. *The Real Thing*. Winchester, Mass.: Faber and Faber, 1984. [ISBN 0-571-12529-8]

_____. *Rock 'n' Roll*. first American edition. New York, N.Y.: Grove Press, 2006. [ISBN 10: 978-0-8021-4307-5, ISBN 13: 0-8021-4307-5]

_____. *Rosencrantz and Guildenstern are Dead*. New York, N.Y.: Grove Press, 1967, seventh printing. [Evergreen Black Cat Book B-162, Library of Congress Catalog Card No. 67-30108]

SOURCES CITED IN THIS BOOK

Brantley, Ben. *New York Times*. April 26, 2004

Delaney, Paul. *Tom Stoppard: Chronology*. Taken from *The Cambridge Companion to Tom Stoppard*. Cambridge, UK: Cambridge University Press, 2001.

_____. Exit Tomas Straussler, enter Sir Tom Stoppard. *Taken from The Cambridge Companion to Tom Stoppard.* Cambridge, UK: Cambridge University Press, 2001.

Reiter, Amy. Salon.com People: Tom Stoppard. http://archive.salon.com/people/bc/2001/11/13/tom_stoppard/print.html (2001)

Riddell, Mary. *New Statesman* Interview, Tom Stoppard. http://www.newstatesman.com/200207080012 (2002)

Simon, John. *New York Magazine* http://nymag.com/nymetro/arts/theater/reviews/n_10327

Tom Stoppard at the *Complete Review.* http://www.complete-review.com/authors/stoppard.htm (author and date unknown)

Awards

"And the winner is . . . "

	PULITZER PRIZE	TONY AWARD	NY DRAMA CRITICS CIRCLE AWARD		
			Best American	Best Foreign	Best Play
1966	No Award	Peter Weiss *Marat / Sade*	Peter Weiss *Marat / Sade*		
1967	Edward Albee *A Delicate Balance*	Harold Pinter *The Homecoming*	Harold Pinter *The Homecoming*		
1968	No Award	Tom Stoppard *Rosencrantz and Guildenstern Are Dead*	Tom Stoppard *Rosencrantz and Guildenstern Are Dead*		
1969	Howard Sackler *The Great White Hope*	Howard Sackler *The Great White Hope*	Howard Sackler *The Great White Hope*		
1970	Charles Gordone *No Place to Be Somebody*	Frank McMahon *Borstal Boy*	Paul Zindel *The Effect of Gamma Rays on Man-in-the-Moon Marigolds*	No Award	Frank McMahon *Borstal Boy*
1971	Paul Zindel *The Effect of Gamma Rays on Man-in-the-Moon Marigolds*	Anthony Shaffer *Sleuth*	John Guare *The House of Blue Leaves*	No Award	David Storey *Home*
1972	No Award	David Rabe *Sticks and Bones*	No Award	Jean Genet *The Screens*	Jason Miller *That Championship Season*
1973	Jason Miller *That Championship Season*	Jason Miller *That Champion Season*	Lanford Wilson *The Hot L Baltimore*	No Award	David Storey *The Changing Room*
1974	No Award	Joseph A. Walker *The River Niger*	Miguel Piñero *Short Eyes*	No Award	David Storey *The Contractor*
1975	Edward Albee *Seascape*	Peter Shaffer *Equus*	Ed Bullins *The Taking of Miss Janie*	No Award	Peter Shaffer *Equus*

	PULITZER PRIZE	TONY AWARD	NY DRAMA CRITICS CIRCLE AWARD		
			Best American	Best Foreign	Best Play
1976	Marvin Hamlisch, music Edward Kleban, lyrics Nicholas Dante, book James Kirkwood, book *A Chorus Line*	Tom Stoppard *Travesties*	David Rabe *Streamers*	No Award	Tom Stoppard *Travesties*
1977	Michael Cristofer *The Shadow Box*	Michael Cristofer *The Shadow Box*	David Mamet *American Buffalo*	No Award	Simon Gray *Otherwise Engaged*
1978	Donald L. Coburn *The Gin Game*	Hugh Leonard *Da*	Hugh Leonard *Da*		
1979	Sam Shepard *Buried Child*	Bernard Pomerance *The Elephant Man*	Bernard Pomerance *The Elephant Man*		
1980	Lanford Wilson *Talley's Folly*	Mark Medoff *Children of a Lesser God*	No Award	Harold Pinter *Betrayal*	Lanford Wilson *Talley's Folly*
1981	Beth Henley *Crimes of the Heart*	Peter Shaffer *Amadeus*	Beth Henley *Crimes of the Heart*	No Award	Athol Fugard *A Lesson from Aloes*
1982	Charles Fuller *A Soldier's Play*	David Edgar *The Life and Adventures of Nicholas Nickleby*	Charles Fuller *A Soldier's Play*	No Award	David Edgar *The Life and Adventures of Nicholas Nickleby*
1983	Marsha Norman *Night, Mother*	Harvey Fierstein *Torch Song Trilogy*	No Award	David Hare *Plenty*	Neil Simon *Brighton Beach Memoirs*
1984	David Mamet *Glengarry Glen Ross*	Tom Stoppard *The Real Thing*	David Mamet *Glengarry Glen Ross*	No Award	Tom Stoppard *The Real Thing*
1985	Stephen Sondheim, music/lyrics James Lapine, book *Sunday in the Park with George*	Neil Simon *Biloxi Blues*	August Wilson *Ma Rainey's Black Bottom*		
1986	No Award	Herb Gardener *I'm Not Rappaport*	Michael Frayn *Benefactors*	No Award	Sam Shepard *A Lie of the Mind*
1987	August Wilson *Fences*	August Wilson *Fences*	No Award	Christopher Hampton *Les Liaisons Dangereuses*	August Wilson *Fences*

	PULITZER PRIZE	TONY AWARD	NY DRAMA CRITICS CIRCLE AWARD		
			Best American	Best Foreign	Best Play
1988	Alfred Uhry *Driving Miss Daisy*	David Henry Hwang *M. Butterfly*	No Award	Athol Fugard *Road to Mecca*	August Wilson *Joe Turner's Come and Gone*
1989	Wendy Wasserstein *The Heidi Chronicles*	Wendy Wasserstein *The Heidi Chronicles*	No Award	Brian Friel *Aristocrats*	Wendy Wasserstein *The Heidi Chronicles*
1990	August Wilson *The Piano Lesson*	Frank Galati *The Grapes of Wrath*	No Award	Peter Nichols *Privates on Parade*	August Wilson *The Piano Lesson*
1991	Neil Simon *Lost in Yonkers*	Neil Simon *Lost in Yonkers*	No Award	Timberlake Wertenbaker *Our Country's Good*	John Guare *Six Degrees of Separation*
1992	Robert Schenkkan *The Kentucky Cycle*	Brian Friel *Dancing at Lughnasa*	August Wilson *Two Trains Running*	No Award	Brian Friel *Dancing at Lughnasa*
1993	Tony Kushner *Angels in America: Millennium Approaches*	Tony Kushner *Angels in America: Millennium Approaches*	No Award	Frank McGuinness *Someone Who'll Watch Over Me*	Tony Kushner *Angels in America: Millennium Approaches*
1994	Edward Albee *Three Tall Women*	Tony Kushner *Angels in America: Perestroika*	Edward Albee *Three Tall Women*		
1995	Horton Foote *The Young Man From Atlanta*	Terrence McNally *Love! Valour! Compassion!*	Terrence McNally *Love! Valour! Compassion!*	No Award	**Tom Stoppard** *Arcadia*
1996	Jonathan Larson *Rent*	Terrence McNally *Master Class*	No Award	Brian Friel *Molly Sweeney*	August Wilson *Seven Guitars*
1997	No Award	Alfred Uhry *The Last Night of Ballyhoo*	No Award	David Hare *Skylight*	Paula Vogel *How I Learned to Drive*
1998	Paula Vogel *How I Learned to Drive*	Yasmina Reza *Art*	Tina Howe *Pride's Crossing*	No Award	Yasmina Reza *Art*
1999	Margaret Edson *Wit*	Warren Leight *Side Man*	No Award	Patrick Marber *Closer*	Margaret Edson *Wit*

	PULITZER PRIZE	TONY AWARD	NY DRAMA CRITICS CIRCLE AWARD		
			Best American	**Best Foreign**	**Best Play**
2000	Donald Margulies *Dinner with Friends*	Michael Frayn *Copenhagen*	No Award	Michael Frayn *Copenhagen*	August Wilson *Jitney*
2001	David Auburn *Proof*	David Auburn *Proof*	David Auburn *Proof*	No Award	Tom Stoppard *The Invention of Love*
2002	Suzan-Lori Parks *Topdog/Underdog*	Edward Albee *The Goat: or, Who Is Sylvia?*	Edward Albee *The Goat: or, Who Is Sylvia?*		
2003	Nilo Cruz *Anna in the Tropics*	Richard Greenburg *Take Me Out*	No Award	Alan Bennett *Talking Heads*	Richard Greenburg *Take Me Out*
2004	Doug Wright *I Am My Own Wife*	Doug Wright *I Am My Own Wife*	Lynn Nottage *Intimate Apparel*		
2005	John Patrick Shanley *Doubt, a Parable*	John Patrick Shanley *Doubt, a Parable*	No Award	Martin McDonagh *The Pillowman*	John Patrick Shanley *Doubt, a Parable*
2006	No Award	Alan Bennet *The History Boys*	Alan Bennett *The History Boys*		
2007	David Lindsay-Abaire *Rabbit Hole*	**Tom Stoppard** *The Coast of Utopia*	August Wilson *Radio Gulf*	No Award	Tom Stoppard *The Coast of Utopia*
2008	Tracy Letts *August: Osage County*	Tracy Letts *August: Osage County*	Tracy Letts *August: Osage County*		

INDEX

absurd (ity) (ism) 7, 8, 9, 10, 11, 13, 14, 22, 32, 37

adaptation (s) 22, 23

Amnesty International 18

Arcadia 30, 31, 32, 33, 34

Artist Descending a Staircase 10

Beckett, Samuel 6, 7

Berman, Ed 18

Broadway 13, 24, 27, 33

Bukovsky, Vladimir 18, 19

Christie, Agatha 8

The Coast of Utopia 34, 35, 36, 37

Cold War 27

custody 9

Czech (oslovakia) (Republic) 1, 2, 18, 19, 21, 22, 37

Dalliance 22

Death of a Salesman 4

dialogue 9, 11, 12, 14, 18, 19, 20, 23, 25, 31, 32, 33

Dirty Linen 17, 18

divorce 10, 11, 29

Dogg's Hamlet, Cahoot's Macbeth 21, 22

Dogg's Our Pet 11, 21

Duchamp, Marcel 10

Eastern Europe (an) 1, 18, 19, 22

Edinburgh Fringe Festival 5

England 2, 5

Enter a Free Man 4, 7

entropy 30

Every Good Boy Deserves Favour 19

Ewing, Kenneth 4, 5

experimental theater 10

farce (s) 9, 10, 17, 23

Feminism 17

The 15-Minute Hamlet 11, 21

Flowering Cherry 4

Hamlet 3, 4

Hapgood 27, 28, 29, 30, 31

Havel, Vaclav 18, 19, 21, 37

Herzen, Alexander 34

homosexual (ity) 33, 34

The Importance of Being Earnest 14, 16

In the Native State 29

India 2, 29

Ingle, Jose 5, 9, 10

The Invention of Love 32, 33, 34

Jewish 1, 2

Jumpers 11, 12, 13, 14, 33

Kendal, Felicity 24, 27, 28, 29

KGB 19

The entries in the index include highlights from the main In an Hour essay portion of the book.

Le Carré, John 27
Lenin, Vladimir 14
London 8, 27, 33

math (ematical) 27, 28, 30, 31
Monty Python 10
Moore-Robinson, Dr. Miriam 9, 10, 11, 14, 17, 24
The Mousetrap 8
music (al) 12, 27, 35, 37
mystery 10, 11

the National Theatre 5, 6
naturalism 13, 25
Nestroy, Johann 23
New-Found-Land 18
Night and Day 19, 20, 21, 24, 31

Off-Broadway 10, 11
the Old Vic Theatre 5, 8, 12
On the Razzle 23, 24, 29
one-act (s) 5, 7, 8, 9, 11, 14
Orton, Joe 10, 12, 18
O'Toole, Peter 3, 4

physics 27
Pirandello, Luigi 6
plot 8, 9, 10, 11, 12, 13, 14, 17, 18, 21, 23, 27, 30, 31, 32, 33
politics 11, 18, 22, 24, 27, 34, 35, 37

The Real Inspector Hound 8, 9, 10
The Real Thing 24, 25, 27, 37
revolution 17, 34, 35, 36

Rock 'n' Roll 37
romance 3, 24, 28, 29
Rosencrantz and Guildenstern Meet King Lear 5
Royal Shakespeare Company 5
Russia (n) 16, 18, 19, 28, 29, 34, 35, 36

Salvage 35, 36
Schnitzler, Arthur 23
Shakespeare 3, 9, 21
Shakespeare in Love 29, 32, 33, 34
Shipwreck 35, 36
Singapore 1
social commentary 7
speech (es) 6, 11, 12, 14, 23, 29, 33, 35
spy 28

television 4, 10, 14, 17
Tony Award 34, 35
Travesties 14, 16, 17, 18, 33
Tzara, Tristan 14, 15, 16

Undiscovered Country 22

Voyage 35

Waiting for Godot 6
A Walk on the Water 3, 4
Western Daily Press 3
Wilde, Oscar 9, 14, 15, 17, 23, 33, 34
World War II 7

ABOUT THE AUTHOR

Mikhail Alexeeff received his B.A. from University California–Santa Cruz and his M.F.A. from UCLA. He has written several award-winning plays that have been performed in the San Francisco Bay Area and in Los Angeles, including *Punching Rabbits* and *Make Angry Love to the Fish*. This is his first biographical work.

NOTE FROM THE PUBLISHER

In an Hour Books LLC would like to thank Farrar, Straus & Giroux, whose enlightened permissions policy reflects an understanding that copyright law is intended both to protect the rights of creators of intellectual property and to encourage its use for the public good.

Know the playwright,
love the play.

Open a new door to theater study, performance, and
audience satisfaction with these Playwrights In an Hour titles.

ANCIENT GREEK

Aeschylus   Aristophanes   Euripides   Sophocles

RENAISSANCE

William Shakespeare

MODERN

Anton Chekhov   Noël Coward   Lorraine Hansberry
Henrik Ibsen   Arthur Miller   Molière   Eugene O'Neill
Arthur Schnitzler   George Bernard Shaw   August Strindberg
Frank Wedekind   Oscar Wilde   Thornton Wilder
Tennessee Williams

CONTEMPORARY

Edward Albee   Alan Ayckbourn   Samuel Beckett
Theresa Rebeck   Sarah Ruhl   Sam Shepard   Tom Stoppard
August Wilson

To purchase or for more information
visit our web site inanhourbooks.com